WHO'S WHO
IN INTERNATIONAL
GOLF

D0877701

WHO'S WHO
IN INTERNATIONAL
GOLF

EDITED BY DAVID EMERY

SPHERE

SPHERE BOOKS LIMITED

30–32 Gray's Inn Road, London WC1X 8JL

First published in Great Britain by
Sphere Books Ltd. 1983
Copyright © First Editions (Rambletree Ltd.) 1983

Edited, designed and produced by First Editions (Rambletree Ltd.)

SPHERE

Set in Sabon by Inforum Ltd, Portsmouth

Printed and bound in Italy by
New Interlitho SpA.

Introduction

Golf, the game that a child can play but an adult never master, has attracted more than its fair share of outstanding individuals over the years. The great names run like a thread of gold though its history: Jones, Hogan, Palmer, Player, Nicklaus . . .

But in the past ten years or so, as the sport has boomed all round the world, an army of virtual unknowns has sprung up to compete for the massive prize money on offer.

Every so often one of the anonymous bunch breaks clear, wins a major title and is transformed into a famous name. The failure rate, though is equally high, especially in America where young hopes burn bright for a year and then drop into oblivion.

The Who's Who in International Golf is designed to keep you up to date with the changing face of the sport. It details all the established stars who are still playing and takes a look at the exciting young talent hoping to take over from them.

The leading women professionals are also included, all listed alphabetically for ease of reference.

Tommy Aaron

Tommy Aaron

Born: February 22, 1937, Gainesville, Georgia, U.S.A.
Lives: Gainesville.
Height: 6–1. *Weight:* 180.
Turned Pro: 1960.
Career Highlights
U.S. Masters: 1973.
Canadian Open: 1969.
Atlanta Classic: 1970.
Walker Cup: 1959.
Ryder Cup: 1969, 1973.
Western Amateur: 1960.

After a good amateur record of runner up in the U.S. Amateur in 1958 and a Walker Cup appearance, Aaron has spent over 20 years on the circuit. He waited a long time for his first victory, coming second nine times before winning the Canadian Open in 1969. His only other tour victory apart from the 1973 Masters is the 1970 Atlanta Classic. The bespectacled Aaron, married to Jimmye and with two children, enjoys bird hunting and fishing.

Amy Alcott

Born: February 22, 1956, Kansas City, Missouri, U.S.A.
Lives: Santa Monica, California.
Height: 5–7. *Weight:* 130.
Turned Pro: 1975.
Career Highlights
U.S. Open: 1980.
LPGA Classic: 1976.
Colgate Far East Open: 1976.
Peter Jackson Classic: 1979.

Voted Player of the Year by America's Golf Magazine in 1980 after her U.S. Open win, Amy is one of the hardest workers on the U.S. tour, constantly practising in an effort to improve her game. She is capable of great birdie streaks. Her U.S. Open triumph was accomplished by only nine strokes.

Amy Alcott.

Peter Alliss

Born: February 28, 1931, Berlin,
Germany.
Lives: Hazelmere, Surrey, England.
Height: 6–0. *Weight:* 212.
Turned Pro: 1946.
Career Highlights
Spanish Open: 1956, 1958.
Italian Open: 1958.
Portuguese Open: 1958.
Ryder Cup: 1953, 1957, 1959, 1961,
1963, 1965, 1967, 1969.

Now a superb television commentator
on both sides of the Atlantic, Alliss followed the famous Henry Longhurst as
the BBC's voice of golf and has a
sparkling reputation as a raconteur and
author. Born in Germany, where his
father, Percy, was a professional, he
was rated one of the greatest strikers of
the ball on the European circuit, but he
possessed a fatal putting flaw.

He returned after an eight-year gap
to appear in the 1982 British Seniors'
Championship and displayed exactly
the same putting problem. He is also a
course designer with Dave Thomas.

Isao Aoki

Born: August 31, 1942, Abiko, Japan.
Lives: Yokohama, Japan.
Height: 5–11. *Weight:* 160.
Turned Pro: 1964.
Career Highlights
World Match Play: 1978; runner up
1979.

Aoki has had 30 victories in Japan and
on the Asian circuits. A brilliant if unor-
thodox putter, he has had several high
placings on hit-and-run raids to
America and Europe. He won the 1978
World Match Play at Wentworth, beating the New Zealander Simon Owen.
He was beaten in the final the following

Isoa Aoki.

year by Bill Rogers. He relaxes by fishing and is married to Hiroko, with a
daughter Joanne.

George Archer

Born: October 1, 1939, San Francisco,
California, U.S.A.
Lives: Gilroy, California.
Height: 6–5. *Weight:* 200.
Turned Pro: 1964.
Career Highlights
U.S. Masters: 1969.
Greensboro: 1967, 1972.
Bing Crosby: 1969.
Pensacola: 1968.
New Orleans: 1968.
Los Angeles: 1972.
San Diego: 1971.
Hartford: 1971.

One of the unluckiest players on the American tour, Archer twice needed major surgery and claims to have started only two years 100 per cent fit since turning pro in 1964. He is recognised to have the most consistent putting stroke and in the 1980 Sea Pines Heritage Classic set an all-time tour low with 94 putts – five fewer than anybody else.

George's first trip to the operating theatre was in 1975, when he tore a tendon in his left wrist. Four years later he was there again when two discs fused in his back.

Archer began playing at 12 and was an outstanding amateur, winning three Californian titles in 1963 and reaching the semis of the U.S. Amateur. He had his finest hour in 1969, when he held on to take the U.S. Masters green jacket against the challenge of Billy Casper and Tom Weiskopf.

Hugh Baiocchi

Born: August 17, 1946, Johannesburg, South Africa.
Lives: Johannesburg.
Height: 6–0. *Weight:* 175.
Turned Pro: 1971.
Career Highlights
Swiss Open: 1973, 1979.
Scandinavian Enterprise Open: 1976.
South African Open: 1978.
Dutch Open: 1975.
Sun Alliance PGA Match Play: 1977.
Zimbabwe Open: 1980.
South African PGA: 1980.

The 1970 South African amateur champion soon became a fairly consistent winner after turning professional, but his form has slumped over the past two years. His lowest round is the 63 he shot in the Hagerman Invitation event in 1971. He competed in the World Cup in 1973, 1977 and 1979.

Hugh Baiocchi.

11

Severiano Ballesteros

Born: April 9, 1957, Pedrena, Spain.
Lives: Pedrena.
Height: 6–0. *Weight:* 192.
Turned Pro: 1974.
Career Highlights
British Open: 1979.
U.S. Masters: 1981.
Dutch Open: 1976, 1980.
French Open: 1977.
Swiss Open: 1977, 1978.
German Open: 1978.
Japanese Open: 1977, 1978.
Spanish Open: 1981.

Greensboro: 1978.
Martini International: 1978, 1980.
Suntory World Match Play
   Championship: 1981, 1982.
Australian PGA: 1981.
Italian Open: 1982.
Madrid Open: 1980, 1982.
Ryder Cup: 1981.

Severiano Ballesteros.

The most excitingly explosive talent to emerge from Europe, Ballesteros has the potential to dominate the world game. Already his popularity among the galleries – if not the organisers – is enormous. His eagerness to attack emulates Arnold Palmer at his best, his ready smile and fractured English make him a worldwide favourite and he has already chalked up victories in Asia, Europe, Africa, Australia and America.

There is still no hint of how good he will become, because whatever happens to his game, his powers of recovery are well known. His wayward driving on the way to winning the 1979 British Open earned him the title of 'The Car Park Golfer.' It prompted Jack Nicklaus to remark: *'Sevvy hits his first and then sees whether he can play his second.'* He topped the European Order of Merit for three successive seasons in 1976, 1977 and 1978 and was second in 1979.

Although he began the 1982 season by claiming the Italian and Madrid Opens, he failed in his stated ambition of winning at least one of the four majors. But he easily earned his exemption for the 1983 American tour with over 100,000 dollars, helped by coming second in the Kemper Open and joint third in the Masters. And he again showed his liking for man-to-man combat by taking the Suntory World Match Play title for the second successive year, beating Britain's Sandy Lyle on the first play-off hole.

Ballesteros winning the British Open 1979.

Brian Barnes.

Miller Barber

Born: March 31, 1931, Shreveport,
  Louisiana, U.S.A.
Lives: Sherman, Texas.
Height: 5–11. *Weight:* 215.
Turned Pro: 1959.
Career Highlights
World Open: 1973.
Ryder Cup: 1969, 1971.
Phoenix: 1971, 1978.
Tucson: 1972.
New Orleans: 1970.

The highlight of Barber's 11 tour victories was the inaugural World Open in 1973, which was then the world's richest tournament with prize money of 500,000 dollars. His reward after eight rounds was 100,000 dollars. He was the famous Mr X in a series of magazine instruction articles. Now mainly on the Seniors' tour, he won the 1982 U.S. Seniors with a final round 65 at Portland, Oregon. One of the shrewdest players around, Miller graduated from the University of Arkansas with a degree in business studies. An American football fanatic, he is married to Karen and they have five children.

Brian Barnes

Born: June 3, 1945, Addington, Surrey,
  England.
Lives: Addington.
Height: 6–2. *Weight:* 217.
Turned Pro: 1964.
Career Highlights
Coca Cola Young Professionals: 1969.
Australian Wills Masters: 1970.
Martini International: 1972.
Dutch Open: 1974.
French Open: 1975.
Sun Alliance Match Play: 1976.
Spanish Open: 1978.
Italian Open: 1979.

Portuguese Open: 1979.
Zambian Open: 1979, 1981.
Kenyan Open: 1981.
Haig Tournament Players'
  Championship: 1981.
Ryder Cup: 1969, 1971, 1973, 1975,
  1977, 1979.

Barnes is one of the most flamboyant characters on the tour with a large pipe clenched between his teeth and obligatory shorts in warm weather. In 1982, he made his silent protest against slow play by sitting on a camp stool between shots. He makes no secret that he dislikes slow rounds and is always threatening to pack in the tour and go fishing – the great passion of his life. Midway though the 1982 season he gave himself only another 18 months.
   An Anglo-Scot, he was brought up in the West country and won the local amateur tournaments and then the British Youths' Championship in 1964. Apart from his first two seasons, he has easily made the top twenty of the European circuit. One of the biggest hitters in the game, he has shown boredom with the tournament schedule before and his sometimes erratic behaviour has infuriated officials. He set a European record in 1980 by winning almost £39,000 for fifth place in the money list without a victory. He is the son-in-law of the 1951 British Open Champion, Max Faulkner.

Dave Barr

Born: March 1, 1952, Kelowna, British
  Columbia, Canada.
Lives: Richmond, British Columbia.
Height: 6–1. *Weight:* 180.
Turned Pro: 1974.
Career Highlights
Topped Canadian Order of Merit:
  1977.

Washington State Open: 1977.
Quad Cities Open: 1981.
Canada World Cup Team: 1977, 1978.

Although the best Canadian player since George Knudson, Barr found it much harder going south of the border. His one tour win was the 1981 Quad Cities Open, when a five-way play-off ended at the eighth extra hole. The powerful Barr is a keen follower of all sports and has a natural eye for the ball. Married to Lu Ann, with a son, Brent.

Andy Bean

Born: March 13, 1953, Lafayette,
  Georgia, U.S.A.
Lives: Grenelefe, Florida.
Height: 6–4. *Weight:* 210.

Andy Bean.

15

Turned Pro: 1975.
Career Highlights
Doral Eastern Open: 1977.
Dunlop Phoenix, Japan: 1978.
Kemper Open: 1978.
Western Open: 1978.
Atlanta: 1979.
Hawaiian Open: 1980.
Bay Hill Classic: 1981.

Bean turned pro in 1975 and gained his first win two years later in the Doral-Eastern Open. He was born into the game: his father was associated with a golf club and when Bean was 15 the family bought a course in Florida. Bean was able to practise as and when he wanted and put the facilities to good use by becoming an outstanding amateur. In 1975, the year he turned pro, he was Western Amateur Champion and a semi-finalist in the national championships. He played a lot of 1981

with a fractured thumb, but still beat Tom Watson by seven strokes to win the Bay Hill Classic.

Frank Beard

Born: May 1, 1939, Dallas, Texas, U.S.A.
Lives: Louisville, Kentucky.
Height: 6–0. *Weight:* 180.
Turned Pro: 1962.
Career Highlights
Tournament of Champions: 1967, 1970.
Texas Open: 1965.
New Orleans Open: 1966, 1971.
Westchester Classic: 1969.
Ryder Cup: 1969, 1971.

Beard has won 11 tour victories, including the Tournament of Champions and the New Orleans Open twice. He was top money winner in 1969, but has not

Maurice Bembridge.

made the top 60 since 1974. His career earnings top the million. He is a keen bridge player.

Maurice Bembridge

Born: February 21, 1945, Worksop, Nottinghamshire, England.
Lives: Iowa, U.S.A.
Height: 5–7.   *Weight:* 170.
Turned Pro: 1960.
Career Highlights
Dunlop Masters: 1971.
Kenyan Open: 1968, 1969, 1979.
German Open: 1975.
Ryder Cup: 1969, 1971, 1973, 1975.
Martini International: 1973.
Benson and Hedges International 1979.

One of the first of the game's globe trotters, Bembridge is now married to an American and his home is in Iowa, although he is reluctant to attack the American circuit. Though erratic, he has shown he is good enough and his brilliant 64 in the last round of the 1974 U.S. Masters equalled the record at Augusta, as did his inward 30. His first national title was the 1968 Kenyan Open and he has won events in New Zealand and Zambia as well as in Europe. He was the leading home player when he finished fifth in the 1968 British Open. His 63 in the pre-qualifying round in the previous year's Open equalled the lowest on record.

Jane Blalock

Born: September 19, 1945, Portsmouth, New Hampshire, U.S.A.
Lives: Highland Beach, Florida.
Height: 5–6.   *Weight:* 120.
Turned Pro: 1969.
Career Highlights
Lady Carling: 1970.

Jane Blalock

Bing Crosby International: 1974.
Orange Blossom Classic: 1978, 1979.
Colgate Triple Crown: 1975, 1977.

The former schoolteacher decided to graduate to the paid sports ranks in 1969 and joined the U.S. women's tour. Since then this one-time outstanding amateur has won more than 30 tournaments and one million dollars. She went 299 events without missing the cut.

John Bland

Born: September 22, 1945,
   Johannesburg, South Africa.
Lives: Johannesburg.
Height: 5–10.   *Weight:* 150.
Turned Pro: 1968.

John Bland.

Career Highlights
Transvaal Open: 1970.
Holiday Inns Champion of
   Champions: 1977.
Victoria Falls Classic: 1977.
Holiday Inns Invitation: 1979.

Bland has been competing off and on in Europe since 1970. Although not a winner, he has been the most consistent South African on the tour in the last six years. In 1981 he tied for fourth in both the Dunlop Masters and the Bob Hope. All his five tournament victories were achieved in South Africa or Zimbabwe. He just failed to win the 1981 South African Open, when even an 18-hole play-off could not divide him and Gary Player. But Player finally took the title on sudden-death holes.

Pat Bradley.

Pat Bradley

Born: March 24, 1951, Westford,
  Massachusetts, U.S.A.
Lives: Marco Island, Florida.
Height: 5–7. *Weight:* 126.
Turned Pro: 1974.
Career Highlights
U.S. Open: 1981.
Girl Talk Classic: 1976.
Bankers Trust Classic: 1977.
Lady Keystone: 1978.
Greater Baltimore Classic: 1980.
Peter Jackson Classic: 1980.
Women's Kemper Open: 1981.

Always a front runner for the big
money, Pat made U.S. Open history in
1981, when she took just 279 strokes to
win the 72-hole tournament. She is well
on her way to making a million dollars
from golf. An outstanding skier in her
spare time.

Gordon Brand

Born: August 6, 1955, Bradford,
  Yorkshire, England.
Lives: Yorkshire.
Height: 5–10. *Weight:* 165.
Turned Pro: 1976.
Career Highlight
Ivory Coast Open: 1981.
Tooting Bec Cup: 1981.

A former English amateur international, Brand has never seriously
threatened to win a major tournament
although he is seldom out of the money.
He finished 19th at the 1981 British
Open at Sandwich, when his second
round 65 included a hole in one at the
16th. It earned him a cheque for £2,012
and the Tooting Bec Cup for the lowest
round by a British player. Gordon's
wife, Lyn, is also a professional golfer
and a member of the WPGA.

Gordon Brand Jnr. winning the Bob Hope Classic 1982.

Gordon Brand Jnr.

Born: August 19, 1958, Kirkcaldy, Scotland.
Lives: Bristol, England.
Height: 5–10. *Weight:* 150.
Turned Pro: 1981.
Career Highlights
English Open Amateur: 1978.
British Youths: 1979.
Scottish Open: 1980.
Coral Welsh Classic: 1982.
Walker Cup: 1979.
Bob Hope Classic: 1982.

Brand was given the 'junior' title by the European tour authorities to distinguish him from his father, the club professional at Knowle, and Yorkshire's Gordon Brand who joined the circuit in 1977. He turned pro after being over-looked for the 1981 Walker Cup, but the reasons for his non-selection proved the foundation of his early success on the tour. The amateur bodies correctly claimed that he was a much better stroke-player than a match-player. He had won the 1979 British Youths' title, the 1978 English Open Amateur and the 1980 Scottish Open – all stroke play events.

His modest target for his first year was a place in the top 60 which he easily attained with victories in the Coral Welsh Classic and the Bob Hope Classic – the first rookie ever to win two events in his first season. He has no ambition to play in America, as he claims he does not like their way of life and does not think he is good enough to be successful there.

Gay Brewer.

Gay Brewer

Born: March 19, 1932, Middletown, Ohio, U.S.A.
Lives: Palm Springs, California.
Height: 6–0. *Weight:* 185.
Turned Pro: 1956.
Career Highlights
U.S. Masters: 1967.
Canadian Open: 1972.
Ryder Cup: 1967, 1973.

The U.S. Junior Champion in 1949, Brewer won 11 U.S. tour victories and many others all over the world including the now-discontinued Alcan Golfer of the Year at St. Andrews in 1967 and Royal Birkdale in 1968. He won the U.S. Masters in 1967, after being third the year before, losing a triple play-off with winner Jack Nicklaus and Tommy Jacobs. In 1966 he was fifth in the money list, but he has been outside the top 150 since 1979.

Tienie Britz

Born: May 14, 1945, Johannesburg, South Africa.
Lives: Johannesburg.
Height: 6–0. *Weight:* 155.
Turned Pro: 1967.
Career Highlights
South African PGA: 1970, 1971.
Natal Open: 1972.
German Open: 1977.

Britz hardly devotes enough time in Europe to be a serious challenge, although he won the 1977 German Open at Dusseldorf. His other victories

Tiene Britz.

have been in his home country and golf now competes with his tomato and flower farm near Johannesburg.

Ken Brown

Born: January 9, 1957, Harpenden, Hertfordshire, England.
Lives: Harpenden.
Height: 6–0. *Weight:* 140.
Turned Pro: 1975.
Career Highlights
Carrolls Irish Open: 1978.
Ryder Cup: 1977, 1979.
World Cup: 1979.

The tall, waif-like figure has been dubbed 'the walking No. 1 iron', but Brown has not yet realised the enormous potential of his sound technique and better-than-average putting. The 1978 Irish Open was thought to be the necessary springboard. Instead the enigmatic Brown collected a £1,000 fine – and temporary suspension from international team events – following misdemeanours in the 1979 Ryder Cup at Greenbrier, West Virginia and his form slumped. He has often brushed with authority and has been fined in the past for slow play. His unconventional – at times downright scruffy – dress has also brought criticism from his fellow pros. But Brown remains his own man, the closest thing to a rebel on the immaculately behaved circuit.

Ken Brown.

George Burns

Born: July 29, 1949, Brooklyn, New York, U.S.A.
Lives: Boynton Beach, Florida.
Height: 6–2.   *Weight:* 190.
Turned Pro: 1975.
Career Highlights
Canadian Amateur: 1973.
Walker Cup Team: 1975.
World Amateur Team: 1975.
Scandinavian Open: 1975.
Kerrygold: 1975.

Burns turned pro in 1975 and had to wait four years before winning the Walt Disney Team Championship with Ben Crenshaw. He seemed set for his first

major in 1981, when he led by three strokes after 54 holes in the United States Open at Merion. But after a last round 73 he tied for second place with Bill Rogers, behind Australian David Graham. A graduate of the University of Maryland with a degree in physical education and recreation, George attended college with the intention of playing plenty of American football, but after a season as a defensive end decided to concentrate on golf.

Bob Byman

Born: April 21, 1955, Poughkeepsie, New York, U.S.A.

George Burns.

Bob Byman.

Lives: Raleigh, North Carolina.
Height: 5–10. *Weight:* 175.
Turned Pro: 1976.
Career Highlights
Bay Hill Citrus Classic: 1979.
New Zealand Open: 1977.
Dutch Open: 1977, 1978.
Scandinavian Open: 1977.

Byman is a physical fitness fanatic who has only one tour victory in the Bay Hill Citrus in 1979, but caused a stir on the European circuit by claiming the Dutch Open in 1977 and 1978 and the Scandinavian Open in 1977. He takes care over what he eats and is regarded on the circuit as a nutrition expert. Married to Michelle, with twins.

Manuel Calero

Born: September 16, 1952, Barcelona, Spain.
Lives: Barcelona.
Height: 5–10. *Weight:* 165.
Turned Pro: 1973.
Career Highlights
Billy Butlin Jersey Open: third 1981.
German Open: eighth 1981.
Tunisian Open: second 1982.
Haig Tournament Players'
  Championship: second 1982.

Calero is one of the busiest players on the European circuit, but has yet to win a tournament. He had the chance to burst the barrier in the first event of the 1982 season, but lost a three-way

Manuel Calero.

play-off in the Tunisian Open to Antonio Garrido. He claimed another second place in the Haig Tournament Players' Championship later in the year.

José-Maria Canizares

Born: February 18, 1947, Madrid, Spain.
Lives: Madrid.
Height: 5–10. *Weight:* 158.
Turned Pro: 1967.
Career Highlights
Bob Hope British Classic: 1980.
Italian Open: 1981.
Ryder Cup: 1981.

The ex-caddy is a phenomenal streak player. That was demonstrated in his second year as a professional when he posted the lowest European nine holes aggregate of 27 in the 1978 Swiss Open. In the same tournament he rolled off 11 successive birdies – five at the end of the second round and six at the start of the third – plus an eagle for a world record. He fired the lowest round of the 1982 European season with a 62 in the Hennessy Cup.

Donna Caponi

Born: January 29, 1945, Detroit, Michigan, U.S.A.

Lives: Los Angeles, California.
Height: 5–5. *Weight:* 120.
Turned Pro: 1965.
Career Highlights
U.S. Open 1969, 1970.
Bluegrass Invitational 1970, 1973.
Peter Jackson Classic: 1976.
Japan Classic: 1976.
Houston Classic: 1978.
LPGA Championship: 1979, 1981.
Colgate-Dinah Shore: 1979.

In 1981 Donna became the third member of the women's tour to top one million dollars prize money, after Kathy Whitworth and JoAnne Carner. A former Los Angeles junior champion, she uses her natural rhythm to good effect on the dance floor.

José-Maria Canizares.

JoAnne Carner

Born: April 4, 1939, Kirkland, Washington, U.S.A.
Lives: Palm Beach, Florida.
Height: 5–7. *Weight:* 133.
Turned Pro: 1970.
Career Highlights
U.S. Amateur: 1957, 1960, 1962, 1966, 1968.
U.S. Open: 1971, 1976.
Colgate Triple Crown: 1978, 1979.

JoAnne's fearless approach to golf has earned her more than 30 titles on the U.S. women's tour and established her as a firm gallery favourite. Five times the U.S. Amateur champion, she was pro Rookie of the Year in her first season of 1970 and has gone on to become

Donna Caponi.

Jo Anne Carner

one of the greats of the women's game. A motorcycle accident threatened her career, but the strawberry blonde who enjoys fishing in the Tennessee mountains, came fighting back. In 1981 she ousted Kathy Whitworth from the top of the all-time money winners with $1,042,544.

Billy Casper

Born: June 24, 1931, San Diego, California, U.S.A.
Lives: Mapleton, Utah.
Height: 5–11.   *Weight:* 200.
Turned Pro: 1954.
Career Highlights
U.S. Open: 1959, 1966.
U.S. Masters: 1970.

Canadian Open: 1967.
Lancome Trophy: 1974.
Italian Open: 1975.
Mexican Open: 1977.
Ryder Cup: 1961, 1963, 1965, 1967, 1969, 1971, 1973, 1975.

Along with Arnie Palmer and Gary Player, Casper caused the golf explosion in the Sixties. He won his first U.S. tour title in Labatt in 1956 and his 50th, the Greater Hartford Open in 1973. When he passed the million dollar prize money mark in 1970, only Palmer had done it before. He was U.S. Player of the Year in 1966 and 1970 and winner of the Vardon Trophy for the best stroke average five times between 1960 and 1968. Casper's winning average in 1968 was a stunning 69.82 and it was twelve years before anyone else (Lee Trevino) went below the 70-stroke barrier. At his peak he was considered the world's best putter and he topped the U.S. prize money list in 1966 and 1968. A Mormon convert in 1966, he henceforward donated 10 per cent of his winnings to that church and lists his interests as religion, family, golf and fishing 'in that order'. He has several allergies and was unable to play golf in Florida because of the turf dressing used in that State. He now devotes his time to the Senior tour – renewing rivalry with Palmer. Married to Shirley, with 11 children.

Roger Chapman

Born: May 1, 1959, Bromley, Kent, England.
Lives: Bromley.
Height: 6–0.   *Weight:* 155.
Turned Pro: 1981.
Career Highlights
English Amateur: 1979.
Walker Cup: 1981.

Chapman had a difficult first year of transition on the tour in 1981, but gained some fame by sharing the first day lead in the Spanish Open. He holed in one at the 16th during the 1981 British Open at Sandwich, when he finished tied 68th.

Bob Charles

Born: March 14, 1936, Carteron, New Zealand.
Lives: New Zealand.
Height: 6–1. *Weight:* 165.
Turned Pro: 1960.
Career Highlights
British Open: 1963.
World Match Play: 1969.
Canadian Open 1968.
New Zealand Open: 1954, 1966, 1970, 1973, 1978.
Swiss Open: 1962, 1974.
South African Open: 1973.
John Player Classic: 1972.
Dunlop Masters: 1972.
Greensboro Open: 1974.
Scandinavian Open: 1973.
Houston Open: 1963.
Atlanta Classic: 1967.

One of the finest putters the game has seen, Charles is certain of a place in history as the first – and so far only – lefthanded British Open champion. He beat American Phil Rodgers in a play-off at Lytham in 1963. He was joint second in the 1968 Open and second again the following year. The tall, elegant Charles, who uses a short, three-quarter backswing with a long follow through, showed his potential by winning the first of his four New Zealand Opens as an amateur in 1954. The last of his five U.S. tour victories was the 1974 Greensboro Open and he devotes his attention these days mainly to the European circuit.

Bob Charles.

Bobby Clampett

Born: April 22, 1960, Monterey, California, U.S.A.
Lives: Carmel Valley Ranch, California.
Height: 5–10. *Weight:* 140.

Turned Pro: 1980.
Career Highlights
California State Amateur: 1978.
Western Amateur: 1978.
Southern Open: 1982.
World Amateur medal: 1978.

Clampett and his distinctive plus two trousers finally cracked the victory barrier in September 1982, when he won the Southern Open in Columbus, Georgia, with four sub-70 rounds. The new 'machine' on the circuit, he shows every sign of being the next superstar.

He started playing tournament golf at the age of 11, and the next year gave up baseball to concentrate on his new love. He is rated to have the best swing since Gene Littler, although Clampett claims there are as many as 52 checkpoints in it. A brilliant amateur and college player, the Barry Manilow look-alike picked up almost 185,000 dollars for 14th place in the money list in his first full season and, although failing to achieve a victory, he finished in second place four times.

He suffered the highs and the lows in the 1982 British Open when rounds of 67 and 66 put him five strokes ahead of

Bobby Clampett.

the field and seven ahead of the eventual winner, Tom Watson. But, after threatening to take Troon apart, he followed with 78 and 77 for a share of tenth place.

He received a French degree at Brigham Young University in 1980 and surprised French journalists by conducting interviews in their language on his first visit to their country in 1981.

Howard Clark
Born: August 26, 1954, Leeds,
   Yorkshire, England.
Lives: Leeds.
Height: 6–0.   *Weight:* 200.
Turned Pro: 1973.
Career Highlights
Portuguese Open: 1978.
Madrid Open: 1978.
Walker Cup: 1973.
Ryder Cup: 1977, 1981.

The husky Yorkshireman's career seemed to be following the right lines when he won the Tournament Players' Under-25 Championship the year after turning professional. Two years later, in 1978, he won the Portuguese and Madrid Open back-to-back. He is still waiting to climb the next plateau, but he put together a fabulous performance in the 1981 Ryder Cup when he shot six birdies and an eagle to demolish Tom Watson four and three. He enjoys the unusual hobby of scripophily – the collecting of old stocks and bonds certificates.

Jim Colbert
Born: March 9, 1941, Elizabeth, New
   Jersey, U.S.A.
Lives: Las Vegas, Nevada.
Height: 5–9.   *Weight:* 165.
Turned Pro: 1965.

Howard Clark.

Career Highlights
Greater Milwaukee Open: 1972.
Greater Jacksonville Open: 1973.
American Golf Classic: 1974.
Tucson Open: 1980.

Colbert was an all-state football player in Kansas, but switched to golf after one year at Kansas State University. He joined the U.S. tour in 1965 and won his first tournament (Monsanto) in 1969. Plagued by knee and back injuries, 1980 was the first year he passed the 100,000 dollar mark. He is a member of the Tour's Tournament Policy Board and graduated from Kansas State University with a degree in political science. Married to Marcia, with three children.

Bobby Cole
Born: May 11, 1948, Springs, South
   Africa.
Lives: Dallas, Texas, U.S.A.
Height: 5–10.   *Weight:* 150.

Turned Pro: 1967.
Career Highlights
British Amateur: 1966.
South African Open: 1975, 1981.
World Cup: 1974.

Cole won the British Amateur when still 18 at Carnoustie, but has since failed to become the South African to follow in the tradition of Bobby Locke and Gary Player. He joined the American tour in 1967 and waited ten years for his only circuit victory – the Buick Open. He represented South Africa three times in the World Cup and won the individual title and, with Dale Hayes, the team prize in the 1974 event. Married to Laura.

Neil Coles

Neil Coles.

Born: September 26, 1934, London, England.
Lives: Weybridge, Surrey.
Height: 5–9. *Weight:* 180.
Turned Pro: 1950.
Career Highlights
PGA Match Play: 1964, 1965, 1973.
Martini International: 1963.
Carrolls: 1965, 1971.
Dunlop Masters: 1966.
Penfold PGA: 1976.
Tournament Players' Championship: 1977.
German Open: 1971.
Spanish Open: 1973.
Ryder Cup: 1961, 1963, 1965, 1967, 1969, 1971, 1973, 1977.

The quiet man of the European golf circuit has been accumulating big cheques ever since he started on the tour in 1957 and would no doubt have gained far more but for a hatred of flying. In 1979 he became the first European to exceed £200,000 in career earnings. He had a quite remarkable record in the now discontinued Daks tournament. He won it twice and tied twice during an eight-year spell, with three of the first places being at Wentworth which he could probably play in the dark. He reached the final of the first World Match Play on the same course in 1964, but lost two and one to Arnold Palmer. He tied second with Johnny Miller in the 1973 British Open and joint third in 1961.

With his froth of white hair, grey slacks and blue sweater, he stands out more than all the young peacocks. A perfect ambassador with such impeccable manners that a rare show of ill-temper in the 1982 British Open provoked an editorial in a leading golf magazine. He has a restricted programme now, but is an energetic Chairman of the European Tournament Players' Committee.

Frank Conner

Born: January 11, 1946, Vienna, Austria.
Lives: San Antonio, Texas, U.S.A.
Height: 5–9. *Weight:* 180.
Turned Pro: 1971.
Career Highlights
U.S. Open: sixth 1981.
New Orleans Open: second 1979.
Quad Cities: second 1981.

Conner won the American National Junior Tennis title at the age of 17 and appeared in three Opens at Forest Hills, but decided to concentrate full-time on golf when he realised he could earn more money. He joined the tour and turned professional in 1971, but did not earn his tour card until three years later. Married to Joy, with two daughters.

Charles Coody

Born: July 13, 1937, Stamford, Texas, U.S.A.
Lives: Abilene, Texas.
Height: 6–2. *Weight:* 185.
Turned Pro: 1963.
Career Highlights
U.S. Masters: 1971.
World Series: 1971.
John Player Classic: 1973.
Ryder Cup: 1971.

Coody is a member of the one million dollars club, but his last big victory was in Scotland where he won the 1973 John Player Classic at Turnberry. He still holds the title as the event was then discontinued. He claimed three U.S. tour victories – 1964 Dallas, 1969 Cleveland and the greatest triumph of

Bobby Cole.

John Cook

all, the 1971 Masters, when he beat Jack Nicklaus and Johnny Miller into second place. Married to Lynett, with three children.

John Cook

Born: October 2, 1957, Toledo, Ohio, U.S.A.
Lives: Dublin, Ohio.
Height: 6–0. *Weight:* 160.
Turned Pro: 1979.
Career Highlights
World Junior Championship: 1974.
U.S. Amateur Championship: 1978.
Bing Crosby National Pro-Am: 1981.

Cook's father convinced him to change to golf from football as he feared his son was too light and might get hurt. He has yet to fulfil his tremendous promise as an amateur. His first tour victory was the 1981 Bing Crosby National Pro-Am after a five-way play-off. Cook has a taste for speed off the course, enjoying motor racing and skiing. His sister

Cathy is a star golfer at Ohio State University, where John studied on the advice of Jack Nicklaus. Married to Jan, with a daughter, Kristin.

Fred Couples

Born: October 3, 1959, Seattle, Washington, U.S.A.
Lives: Palm Springs, California.
Height: 5–11. *Weight:* 185.
Turned Pro: 1980.
Career Highlight
Washington State Open: 1978.

Couples had to choose between baseball and golf in high school as the seasons overlapped. When he really lashes out, his baseball timing is evident. In his first season in 1981 he was the leading rookie money winner with almost 79,000 dollars. He was the low amateur in the 1978 U.S. Open and in contention on the last day of the 1982 event. In the 1982 U.S. PGA, his final round of 66 tied him in third place with

Calvin Peete. His wife, Deborah, is a tennis professional in Palm Springs.

Ben Crenshaw

Born: January 11, 1952, Austin, Texas, U.S.A.
Lives: Austin, Texas.
Height: 5–9. *Weight:* 165.
Turned Pro: 1973.
Career Highlights
Irish Open: 1976.
Hawaiian Open: 1976.
Bing Crosby Pro-Am: 1976.
Phoenix Open: 1979.
Ryder Cup: 1981.

Crenshaw threatened to break every record in the book and the 'Wonder Boy' tag was hung on him even before he turned professional. Before joining the paid ranks, he had finished third in the 1972 Heritage Classic and sixth in the Houston Open. He had a brilliant amateur career and was the winner of the NCAA Championship three straight years 1971, 1972 (tied with Tom Kite) and 1973, for the University of Texas. He earned his tour card in autumn 1973, winning medallist honours by a staggering 12 strokes and, then, in his first start, won the San Antonio-Texas Open by two strokes from Orville Moody.

A keen historian of the game who collects golf artifacts, he seems to try too hard in majors. His temperament must be suspect as he has lost all five play-offs he has been involved in. Married to Poly.

Ben Crenshaw.

Beth Daniel

Born: October 14, Charleston, South
  Carolina, U.S.A.
Lives: Seabrook Island, South
  Carolina.
Height: 5–10. *Weight:* 130.
Turned Pro: 1978.
Career Highlights
U.S. Amateur: 1975, 1977.
Curtis Cup: 1976, 1978.
Patty Berg Classic: 1979, 1980.
Golden Lights: 1980.
Columbia Savings Classic: 1980.
World Championship of Women's
  Golf: 1980, 1981.
Florida Lady Citrus: 1981.

Beth, a brown-eyed blonde competed
for the men's team during her last two
years at University where she graduated
with a degree in education. After a great
amateur career, which included two
U.S. titles, she turned pro and immedi-
ately earned 100,000 dollars in her first
season to win the Rookie of the Year
Award. In 1980 she established a
record for the women's tour in America
by winning 231,000 dollars.

Eamonn Darcy

Born: August 7, 1952, Delgany,
  Ireland.
Lives: Maidenhead, Kent.
Height: 6–1. *Weight:* 182.
Turned Pro: 1969
  Career Highlights
Greater Manchester Open: 1977.
Air New Zealand Open: 1980.
Irish Match Play: 1981.
Kenya Open: 1982.
Ryder Cup: 1975, 1977, 1971.

The Irishman with a peculiar loop at the
top of his swing seems to enjoy the sun
on his back. Although he has won tournaments in Australia, New Zealand,

Eamonn Darcy.

Zambia and Kenya, the Greater Manchester Open in 1977 remains his one
European success. He went close to
winning the 1981 Benson and Hedges,
but was edged out by Tom Weiskopf.

Baldovino Dassu

Born: November 11, 1952, Florence,
  Italy.
Lives: Florence.
Height: 6–2. *Weight:* 155.
Turned Pro: 1971.
Career Highlights
British Youths: 1970.
Italian Open: 1976.
Dunlop Masters: 1976.

Dassu does not give the impression of
working at the game hard enough to
achieve consistency. He announced his
arrival as a professional with an incredible 60 in the 1971 Swiss Open, the
record for the European tour.

Beth Daniel.

Rodger Davis.

Bruce Devlin

Born: October 10, 1937, Armidale, Australia.
Lives: Houston, Texas, U.S.A.
Height: 6–1.   *Weight:* 155.
Turned Pro: 1961.
Career Highlights
Australian Amateur: 1959.
Australian Open: 1960.
French Open: 1963.
New Zealand Open: 1963.
World Cup: 1970.

After winning his national amateur title in 1959, Devlin took the Australian Open Championship the next year, still as an amateur. Starting with the 1964 St. Petersburg Open, he has eight U.S. tour victories. He won the World Cup for his home country with David Graham in 1970. A keen student of the Turf like most Australians, Bruce is also an expert on golf course architecture. Married to Gloria, with three children.

Rodger Davis

Born: May 18, 1951, Sydney, Australia.
Lives: Sydney.
Height: 5–10.   *Weight:* 173.
Turned Pro: 1975.
Career Highlights
South Australian Open: 1978.
State Express Classic: 1981.

The 'nearly' man of the tour and the most dapper, almost always dressed in plus twos, Davis is a big cheque winner but hardly ever a champion. Before his first European victory – the State Express Classic at the Belfry in 1981 – he had been placed second 14 times.

His greatest disappointment was the 1979 British Open at Lytham, where he led with five holes to play, but a disastrous slump for a 73 dropped him to fifth place.

Danny Edwards

Born: June 14, 1951, Ketchcan, Alaska, U.S.A.
Lives: Edmond, Oklomoma.
Height: 5–11.   *Weight:* 155.
Turned Pro: 1973.
Career Highlights
Walt Disney World National Team Championship: 1980.
Greater Greensboro Open: 1977, 1982.
Walker Cup 1973.

Edwards had a magnificent amateur record, but struggled after joining the U.S. tour. His best year was 1977 when he finished 28th on the money list and won the Greater Greensboro Open. He won the 1980 Walt Disney World National Team Championship with his younger brother David. He has recently worked hard on his game again and gained reward with his second Greater Greensboro title in 1982. He is also a racing car driver and in 1981 won three of the 11 races he entered.

David Edwards

Born: April 18, 1956, Neosha, Missouri, U.S.A.
Lives: Edmond, Oklahoma.
Height: 5–8. *Weight:* 155.
Turned Pro: 1978.
Career Highlight
Walt Disney World National Team Championship: 1980.

After winning the NCAA Championship in 1978, Edwards earned his card at the Autumn qualifying school that same year. He is still trying for a top 60 placing, but won the Walt Disney Team Championship in 1980 with his elder brother Danny. He enjoys tinkering with cars and motorbikes. Married to Jonnie.

Danny Edwards.

Dave Eichelberger

Born: September 3, 1943, Waco, Texas, U.S.A.
Lives: Fort Worth, Texas.
Height: 6–1. *Weight:* 180.
Turned Pro: 1966.
Career Highlights
Greater Milwaukee: 1971, 1977.
Bay Hill Classic: 1980.
Tallahassee Open: 1981.
Walker Cup: 1965.

Eichelberger is one of the busiest veterans on the tour, but also one of most erratic, with incredible highs – top eagle scorer with 16 in 1980 – and also embarrassing lows. He admits he should work harder on his game. His first two tour victories were both the Greater Milwaukee, but were separated by six years: 1971 and 1977. A graduate in business administration from Oklamoma State University, Dave is married to Linda, with three children.

Lee Elder

Born: July 14, 1934, Dallas, Texas, U.S.A.
Lives: Washington, D.C.
Height: 5–8. *Weight:* 180.
Turned Pro: 1959.
Career Highlights
Ryder Cup: 1979.
Monsanto: 1974.
Houston Open: 1976.
Greater Milwaukee Open: 1978.
Westchester Classic: 1978.

Perhaps Elder's biggest honour has been making the Negro acceptable on the tour and encouraging others to follow his example. Although a pro since 1959, he did not earn his tour card until the autumn of 1967. His first tournament win was the 1974 Monsanto Open when he beat Britain's Peter Oos-

Lee Elder.

terhuis at the fourth extra hole. His career has been handicapped by a recurrent knee injury – a legacy of his football background. But he ignored it long enough in 1978 to have his best year ever. He beat Lee Trevino on the eighth extra hole of the play-off to take the Greater Milwaukee Open and a month later birdied the final hole of the Westchester Classic to beat Mark Hayes by one shot. For the past 12 years he has hosted the Lee Elder Celebrity Pro-Am, with proceeds going to a scholarship foundation. Lee took a year off the U.S. tour in 1982. Married to Rose.

Pip Elson

Born: April 14, 1954, Kenilworth, Warwickshire, England.
Lives: Coventry.

Height: 5–11.   *Weight:* 168.
Turned Pro: 1972.
Career Highlight
British Youths' Championship: 1971.

European Rookie of the Year in 1973, the well-build Elson has found pro golf a struggle. He manages to qualify, but seldom plays himself into a position to threaten the leaders. His lowest round was a 64 in the 1979 Welsh Classic. He is a member of the European Tour Players' Committee.

Nick Faldo

Born: July 18, 1957, Welwyn Garden City, Hertfordshire, England.
Lives: Hertfordshire.
Height: 6–3.   *Weight:* 192.
Turned Pro: 1976.

Nick Faldo.

Career Highlights
British Youths: 1975.
English Amateur: 1975.
Skol Lager: 1977.
British PGA: 1978, 1980, 1981.
Haig Tournament Players'
  Championship: 1982.
Ryder Cup: 1977, 1979, 1981.

Faldo took up the game as a 13-year-old after watching it on television and thinking it was an easy way to make money. As yet he has not really changed his mind. Within five years he had claimed both the British Youths' and the English Amateur titles and he turned professional in 1976. He finished in the top 60 in 1977 and was named Rookie of the Year that year after collecting his big cheque that year, when he won the Skol Lager Individual. He then began a passionate love affair with the British PGA, winning in 1978, 1980

Nick Faldo.

and 1981. After several high finishes, including joint fourth in the 1982 British Open, he won the Tournament Players' Championship.

He also played 15 tournaments on the American circuit and guaranteed his place on the 1983 tour, helped by big pay-outs in the Canadian Open and the American PGA. His lowest round was 62 in the 1981 Hawaiian Open and obviously he sees his future in America. Married to Melanie, a journalist who went round to interview him for a jogging magazine.

Keith Fergus

Born: March 3, 1954, Temple, Texas, U.S.A.
Lives: Sugarland, Texas.
Height: 6–1. *Weight:* 185.
Turned Pro: 1976.
Career Highlights
Memorial: 1981.
Pacific Atlantic Classic: 1982.
U.S. Amateur: runner up 1975.

Fergus started playing at the age of eight and it is a mystery why this big driver has not had more tour wins. His breakthrough was the Memorial Tournament on challenging Muirfield Village course in Ohio. He won the 1982 Pacific-Atlanta Classic at Georgia. An All American for three years at the University of Houston, Keith was Texas Junior Champion in 1971 and Texas Open Champion in 1976. Married to Cyndy, with a son, Steven.

Vicente Fernandez

Born: April 5, 1946, Buenos Aires, Argentina.
Lives: Buenos Aires.
Height: 5–7. *Weight:* 145.
Turned Pro: 1968.

Vicente Fernandez.

Career Highlights
Argentine Open: 1968, 1969, 1981.
Dutch Open: 1970.
Brazil Open: 1977.
Colgate PGA Championship: 1979.

The compact Argentinian missed the bulk of the European tour in 1982 as a result of the war in the Falklands between Britain and Argentina. He was unable to obtain a visa for Britain until August and had little time to make an impact. His greatest moment remains the 1979 PGA Championship which he won in a fierce wind at St. Andrews.

Ed Fiori
Born: April 21, 1953, Lynwood, California, U.S.A.
Lives: Sugarland, Texas.
Height: 5–7. *Weight:* 175.
Turned Pro: 1977.
Career Highlights
Southern Open: 1979.
Western Open: 1981.
Southern Californian Open: 1981.

Fiori odd-jobbed after high school in construction work, grabbing games of golf whenever he could. In one such game he birdied the last four holes in a tournament in Guadalajara, Mexico, to earn a play-off with Craig Stadler and Jack Rennie. Stadler won the play-off, but a watching member of the University of Houston was impressed and recommended Fiori for a scholarship. In his second year at Houston they won the national collegiate title and Ed was named in the All American team. He dropped out of Houston in 1977 to try his luck on the circuit. Married to Debbie.

Raymond Floyd
Born: September 4, 1942, Fort Bragg, North Carolina, U.S.A.
Lives: Miami, Florida.
Height: 6–1. *Weight:* 200.
Turned Pro: 1961.
Career Highlights
U.S. Masters: 1976.
U.S. PGA: 1969, 1982.

Raymond Floyd.

Canadian PGA: 1981.
World Open: 1976.
Greensboro Open: 1979.
Ryder Cup: 1969, 1975, 1977, 1981.

Floyd is like good wine: he improves with age, coming second on the American money list in 1981 and 1982. The top place in 1982 was denied him by a play-off loss to Craig Stadler in the World Series. Floyd made an instant impact when he won the 1963 St. Petersburg Open as a rookie and, at 20 years and six months, was the third youngest winner on tour. After gaining his first U.S. PGA Championship, the husky giant went six years without a win partly because he developed a taste for *la dolce vita*.

He got back on course with the 1975 Kemper. He claimed the Masters the next year, winning by eight strokes from Ben Crenshaw and his 271 total equalled the tournament record set by Jack Nicklaus in 1965. His reputation as a streak player was emphasised by his display in the 1982 PGA, when he set a tournament record with a 200 total for 54 holes. He also picked up the Memorial and Memphis Classic in 1982. His best performance in the British Open was joint second behind Nicklaus in 1978 at St. Andrews. He has now earned more than two million dollars prize money after leaving the University of North Carolina. Married to Maria, with three children.

Bernard Gallacher

Born: February 9, 1949, Bathgate, Scotland.
Lives: Wentworth, Berkshire.
Height: 5–9. *Weight:* 168.
Turned Pro: 1967.
Career Highlights

Spanish Open: 1977.
French Open: 1979.
Dunlop Masters: 1974, 1975.
Carrolls International: 1974.
Haig Tournament Players'
    Championship: 1980.
Greater Manchester Open: 1981.
Martini International: 1971, 1982.
Jersey Open: 1982.
Ryder Cup: 1969, 1971, 1973, 1975,
    1977, 1979, 1981.

Gallacher has been a most dangerous competitor on the European tour ever since he became the youngest winner of their Order of Merit in 1969 when only 20 – the same year he became the youngest ever member of Britain's Ryder Cup team. He never climbed as high again, but the softly-spoken Scot is

Bernard Gallacher.

Angel Gallardo.

a consistent winner even though he now combines the circuit with the job as club professional at Wentworth. He claimed two victories in 1982 – his second Martini triumph and then the Jersey Open after a play-off with Bill Longmuir.

Angel Gallardo
Born: July 29, 1943, Barcelona, Spain.
Lives: Barcelona.
Height: 5–7. *Weight:* 160.
Turned Pro: 1962.
Career Highlights
Spanish Open: 1970.
Portuguese Open: 1967.
Italian Open: 1977.
Mexican Open: 1971.

Gallardo is still capable of stringing together a series of good scores, although he combines playing with golf journalism for Spanish newspapers.

Antonio Garrido

Born: February 2, 1944, Madrid,
  Spain.
Lives: Madrid.
Height: 5–8. *Weight:* 155.
Turned Pro: 1961.
Career Highlights
Spanish Open: 1972.
Madrid Open: 1977.
Tunisian Open: 1982.
Ryder Cup: 1979.

Garrido took a flier at the 1982 season
by winning the Tunisian Open, the first
tournament of the European circuit. He
followed with a third in the next tournament in Madrid, but failed to sustain
the sparkling pace. An ex-caddy, he had
the distinction, along with compatriot
Sevvy Ballesteros, of being the first
Continentals to play in the Ryder Cup
when the British team was expanded to
take in Europe in 1979.

Al Geiberger

Born: September 1, 1937, Red Bluff,
  California, U.S.A.
Lives: Santa Barbara, California.
Height: 6–2. *Weight:* 176.
Turned Pro: 1959.
Career Highlights
PGA Championship: 1966.
Ontario Open: 1962.
American Golf Classic: 1965.
Tournament of Champions: 1975.
Tournament Players' Championship:
  1975.
Greensboro Open: 1976.
Western Open: 1976.
Ryder Cup: 1967, 1975.

Geiberger is one of the most courageous
sportsmen in the world: his continued
presence on tour is a credit to American
surgery and his own indomitable
spirit, for he has undergone six major
operations. Just how great a player

Geiberger might have become with
normal health was shown in the second
round of the 1977 Danny Thomas-
Memphis Classic, when he became the
first ever to break 60 in an official tour
event. He scored a 13-under par 59
with 11 birdies and one eagle, needing
only 23 putts. The Ontario Open in
1962 was the first of 11 tour successes.
Married to Lynn, with five children, Al
is a keen amateur photographer.

Gibby Gilbert

Born: January 14, 1941, Chattanooga,
  Tennessee, U.S.A.
Lives: Chattanooga.
Height: 5–9. *Weight:* 182.
Turned Pro: 1964.
Career Highlights
Houston Open: 1970.
Danny Thomas-Memphis Classic:
  1976.
Walt Disney World National Team
  Championship: 1977.

Gilbert is one of the many consistent
money winners and owed his exempt
status on the 1982 U.S. tour to being
among the top 50 in career earnings.
The first of his three tour victories was
at Houston back in 1970. In 1977 he
and Grier Jones won the Walt Disney
World National Team Championship.
Gibby was born with initials only –
C.L. Gilbert, Jnr – but that didn't stop
him making an impact as soon as he
started golf at the age of 13. Married to
Judy, with three children.

Bob Gilder

Born: December 31, 1950, Corvallis,
  Oregon, U.S.A.
Lives: Corvallis, Oregon.
Height: 5–9. *Weight:* 165.
Turned Pro: 1973.
Career Highlights

Al Geiberger.

Phoenix Open: 1976.
Canadian Open: 1980.
New Zealand Open: 1974.
Byron Nelson Classic: 1982.
Manufacturers' Hanover Classic: 1982.
Boston Classic: 1982.

Gilder needed four attempts to earn his tour card in 1975 and while he was waiting he picked up the New Zealand Open in 1974. He was quite happy to miss out on star status as he wanted to enjoy individual privacy, but that vanished when he caught fire in 1982 with three victories. He won the Byron Nelson Classic and then the Manufacturers' Hanover Classic after a play-off with Peter Jacobsen. He equalled the all-time PGA tour record for the first 54 holes with an 18-under total of 192, first set by Mike Souchak in 1955. He then claimed the Boston Classic. Married to Peggy, with three children.

Stewart Ginn

Born: June 2, 1949, Melbourne, Australia.
Lives: Melbourne.
Height: 5–7. *Weight:* 150.
Turned Pro: 1969.
Career Highlights
Martini International: 1974.
Australian Professional Championship: 1979.
Australian PGA: 1979.
Malaysian Open: 1977.
New Zealand Open: 1979.

Victory in the Martini in 1974 did not signal a breakthrough in Europe and Ginn's main success is still on his native circuit, which he almost monopolised in 1979. He won the Australian PGA and Professional titles plus the New Zealand Open. Like compatriot Rodger Davis, he is one of the tour's sharp dressers, often favouring plus two trousers.

David Graham.

David Graham

Born: May 23, 1946, Windsor, Australia.
Lives: Dallas, Texas, U.S.A.
Height: 5–10. *Weight:* 164.
Turned Pro: 1962.
Career Highlights
PGA Championship: 1979.
U.S. Open: 1981.
World Match Play: 1976.
American Golf Classic: 1976.
Phoenix Open: 1981.
Japan Open: 1971.
Wills Masters 1975.
Australian Open: 1977.
New Zealand Open: 1979.
Mexican Open: 1980.
World Cup: 1970.

Graham started out as a lefthander, but switched round after two years at the age of 16. He became a full-time pro at 18, but three years later was declared bankrupt with business debts of £3,000. He subsequently paid them off with his tournament winnings, which now comfortably top the million dollar mark. Although he lives in Dallas, Graham has retained the Australian love of globetrotting and has won major tournaments in 11 countries. He is renowned for his iron nerves and he needed them for his victories in the PGA and U.S. Open Championships. In the first he double bogeyed the last hole to put him in a play-off with Ben Crenshaw and then, when the pressure was at its toughest, he birdied the third extra hole to win. He came from behind to claim the U.S. Open, hitting all 18 greens in regulation strokes in the last round. He won the World Cup team championship for Australia in 1970 with Bruce Devlin. He takes a keen interest in club design. Married to Maureen, with two sons.

David Graham.

Lou Graham

Born: January 7, 1938, Nashville,
  Tennessee, U.S.A.
Lives: Nashville, Tennessee.
Height: 6–0. *Weight:* 175.
Turned Pro: 1962.
Career Highlights
U.S. Open: 1975.
Ryder Cup: 1973, 1975, 1977.
Minnesota Classic: 1967.
San Antonio – Texas Open: 1979.

Unlucky with injuries and illness
throughout his tour career, Graham has
needed to use the 10-year exemption
from qualifying stemming from his U.S.
Open win in 1975 to stay on the tour. In
his Open triumph, he tied with John
Mahaffey at Medinah and won the
play-off 71 to 73. Lou turned pro after
his discharge from the Army in 1962,
but within five years was troubled by
severe tendonitis. Married to Patsy,
with two daughters.

Hubert Green

Born: December 18, 1946, Nashville,
  Tennessee. U.S.A.
Lives: Shoal Creek, Alabama.
Height: 6–1. *Weight:* 180.
Turned Pro: 1970.
Career Highlights
U.S. Open: 1977.
Ryder Cup: 1977, 1979.
Houston Open: 1971.
Tallahassee Open: 1973.
Jacksonville Open: 1974, 1976.
Hawaiian Open: 1978, 1979.
Irish Open: 1977.

Green earned his first tour victory in
Houston in 1971 when he was named
'Rookie of the Year.' He claimed three
titles in a row in 1976 – the Doral-
Eastern Open, the Greater Jacksonville
Open and the Heritage. Classic. The

Hubert Green.

U.S. Open followed the next year. He
took a peculiar decision in 1980 to bas-
ically re-build his swing, despite 16 tour
victories and several overseas titles. It
was a disaster and he returned to the
victory trail in the 1981 Sammy Davis
Jr. – Greater Hartford Open by revert-
ing to his old style. He lists his hobbies
as bridge, antique collecting, nature,
gardening and chess. Married to Karen,
with two sons.

Jay Haas

Born: December 2, 1953, St. Louis,
  Missouri, U.S.A.
Lives: Charlotte, North Carolina.
Height: 5–10. *Weight:* 174.
Turned Pro: 1976.
Career Highlights
Walker Cup 1975.
Hall of Fame Classic: 1982.

Texas Open: 1982.
Andy Williams – San Diego Open:
1978.
Greater Milwaukee Open: 1981.

Haas is a nephew of the 1968 Masters
Champion Bob Goalby, who started
Jay playing when he was five. Goalby's
advice helped him win the Illinois State
high school championship in 1972.
After 1975, when he won all three
Walker Cup matches, Jay reached the
fifth round of the British Amateur and
was the low amateur in the U.S. Open,
it was obvious that his next step was the
pro tour. He earned his card at the 1976
autumn school.

After a disappointing first year, he
has steadily increased his standing in
the money list. His first victory was the
1978 Andy Williams-San Diego Open
and in 1982 he followed up by winning
two tournaments – the Hall of Fame
Classic and the Texas Open. At San
Antonio, he beat off the challenge of his
college team-mate and fraternity
brother at Wake Forest University,
Curtis Strange, to win by three strokes.
Married to Janice, with a son, Jay, Jnr.

Dan Halldorson

Born: April 2, 1952, Winnipeg,
Canada.
Lives: Shilo, Manitoba, Canada.
Height: 5–10. *Weight:* 180.
Turned Pro: 1971.
Career Highlights
Pensacola Open: 1980.
World Cup: 1980.
Quebec Open: 1980.

Another Canadian following in the
tradition of George Knudson, Halldorson first qualified in 1974, but he lost
his card after picking up only 619 dollars in 1975. He re-qualified in 1978

with much more success and won his
first tournament – the Pensacola Open
– two years later. In the same year he
won the World Cup for Canada with
Jim Nelford at his third appearance in
the event. As a boy in Winnipeg, Dan
lived across the road from a golf course.
He also built his own practice area in
his back garden. A keen carpenter and
do-it-yourself man, he is married to
Sharon.

Dan Halldorson.

Morris Hatalsky

Born: November 10, 1951, San Diego,
  California, U.S.A.
Lives: Daytana Beach, Florida.
Height: 5–11. *Weight:* 165.
Turned Pro: 1973.
Career Highlights
Hall of Fame Classic: 1981.
Mexican Junior Champion: 1968.

After an outstanding college career,
Hatalsky needed five qualifying schools
before passing in 1976. After a poor
1977, he went to Ken Venturi for help
and encouragement: Venturi changed
his swing and his attitude and Morris
went out in 1981 to win the Hall of
Fame Classic at Pinehurst, after a tussle
with Jerry Pate. He was captain of the
1972 U.S. International University.

  Married to Tracy, with a son, Daniel.

Mark Hayes

Born: July 12, 1949, Stillwater,
  Oklahoma, U.S.A.
Lives: Edmond, Oklahoma.
Height: 5–11. *Weight:* 170.
Turned Pro: 1973.
Career Highlights
Pensacola Open: 1976.
Byron Nelson Classic: 1976.
Tournament Players' Championship:
  1977.
Ryder Cup: 1979.

Hayes took up the game because he was
too small for anything else as a schoolboy. The Tournament Players' Championship in 1977 is his biggest win on the
tour so far. The year before he won the
Byron Nelson Classic and the Pensacola
Open. His second round 63 in the 1977
British Open at Turnberry set a course
record. He is married to Jana.

Mark Hayes.

Sandra Haynie

Born: June 4, 1943, Fort Worth, Texas.
Lives: Dallas, Texas.
Height: 5–5. *Weight:* 120.
Turned Pro: 1961.
Career Highlights
U.S. Open: 1974.
LPGA: 1965, 1974.

With more than 40 tournament victories, Sandra is rightly regarded as one of the outstanding players in the women's game. She was elected to the Ladies Professional Golf Association's Hall of Fame in 1977. She has been an influential figure in the development of women's golf in America, serving on the LPGA Executive Committee.

Vance Heafner

Born: August 11, 1954, Charlotte, North Carolina, U.S.A.
Lives: Raleigh, North Carolina.
Height: 6–0. *Weight:* 170.
Turned Pro: 1978.
Career Highlight
Walt Disney World National Team Championship: 1981.

Heafner had several false starts as a professional after an outstanding college career, but began finishing consistently well in 1980. The following year he won the Walt Disney Team Championship with Mike Holland, with a record-breaking 42-under par – five ahead of the second team. Vance is the son of Clayton Heafner, a fine American player in the Fifties and Sixties. Married to Paige.

Jerry Heard

Born: May 1, 1947, Visalia, California, U.S.A.
Lives: Raleigh, North Carolina.

Height: 6–0. *Weight:* 186.
Turned Pro: 1968.
Career Highlights
American Golf Classic: 1971.
Florida Citrus Open: 1972, 1974.
Spanish Open: 1974.
Atlanta Classic: 1978.

Heard was a dangerous competitor from the time he won his first tour victory – the American Classic – in 1971 until 1976. His fortunes revived in 1978, when he was 29th on the money list and he claimed his fifth tour victory in the Atlanta Classic. Keen on trout fishing and duck hunting, Jerry is married to Phylis.

Harold Henning

Born: October 3, 1934. Johannesburg, South Africa.
Lives: Johannesburg.
Height: 6–2. *Weight:* 175.
Turned Pro: 1953.
Career Highlights
Italian Open: 1957.
Swiss Open: 1960, 1964, 1965.
South African Open: 1957, 1962.
South African PGA: 1965, 1966, 1967, 1972.
German Open: 1965.
Texas Open: 1966.
Dutch Open: 1981.

One of the game's great survivors, Henning proved that age was no barrier when he won the 1981 Dutch Open at 46 – 24 years after claiming his first South African Open success. He won money all over the world including several lucrative years on the American tour.

His best performances in the British Open were separated by a ten-year gap. He tied third in 1960 behind Kel Nagle and Arnold Palmer and occupied the

53

same position with Lee Trevino behind Jack Nicklaus and Doug Sanders in 1970. Both events were at St. Andrews. One of the game's fastest players, Harold won the 1965 World Cup team event with Gary Player. He is one of three brothers, all golfers.

Dave Hill

Born: May 20, 1937, Jackson, Michigan, U.S.A.
Lives: Lakewood, Colorado.
Height: 5–11. *Weight:* 140.
Turned Pro: 1958.
Career Highlights
Danny Thomas-Memphis: 1967, 1969, 1970, 1973.
Houston Open: 1974.
Greater Milwaukee Open: 1976.
Ryder Cup: 1969, 1973, 1977.

Hill is the winner of 13 tour victories but no majors, although he finished second to Tony Jacklin in the 1971 U.S. Open. He almost made the Memphis tournament his own with four wins. He had 17 successive seasons in the top 60, his highest being second in 1969. A nervous player, Dave has been known to lose up to two stone in a season. Obsessed with technical perfection, he wants '*to master the golf ball like Ben Hogan did*'. He won the Vardon Trophy for the lowest stroke average on the tour (70.34) in 1969. He enjoys bridge and is married to Sandie.

Lon Hinkle

Born: July 17, 1949, Flint, Michigan, U.S.A.
Lives: Dallas, Texas.
Height: 6–2. *Weight:* 220.
Turned Pro: 1972.
Career Highlights
New Orleans Open: 1978.

World Series: 1979.
Bing Crosby National Pro-Am 1979.

One of the longest drivers in the game, Hinkle could easily have faded out of golf after winning only 40,000 dollars in his first five years. Improvement started in 1977 and he has topped the century mark every year since. On one of his overseas hit-and-runs raids when things were not going well, he met his beautiful Swiss wife, Edith. Lon's father is an associate professor of Literature at San Diego State University, which explains Lon's love of reading. He was one of seven children who all took up golf and competed in junior tournaments throughout Southern California. In 1980 Lon finished third to Jack Nicklaus in the U.S. Open and PGA Championships − a long way behind, but nevertheless a great boost to his confidence. The following year he exercised his massive frame in the National Long Drive contest, winning with a mighty tee shot of 338 yards six inches.

Scott Hoch

Born: November 24, 1955, Raleigh, North Carolina, U.S.A.
Lives: Raleigh, North Carolina.
Height: 5–11. *Weight:* 170.
Turned Pro: 1979.
Career Highlights
Walker Cup: 1979.
Quad Cities Open: 1980.

After gaining his card in the 1979 autumn school, Hoch jarred his back and missed most of the 1980 season, but then in the 23rd tournament of the year he won the Quad Cities Open after a record first round 63. Despite back problems which have plagued him ever since, he returned to take the USF & G Classic in New Orleans in 1982.

Scott Hoch.

Mike Holland

Born: March 12, 1956, Florence, South
  Carolina, U.S.A.
Lives: Bishopsville, South Carolina.
Height: 5–11. *Weight:* 170.
Turned Pro: 1978.
Career Highlights
Walt Disney World National Team
  Championship: 1981.
South Carolina Amateur Champion:
  1976.

Holland found the transition from
amateur to professional difficult, but he
began to make progress after advice
and coaching from Bert Yancey. He
won the 1981 Walt Disney Team
Championship with Vance Heafner.

Tommy Horton

Born: June 16, 1941, St. Helens,
  Lancashire, England.
Lives: Jersey.
Height: 5–9. *Weight:* 140.
Turned Pro: 1957.
Career Highlights
South African Open: 1970.

55

Tommy Horton.

Nigerian Open: 1973.
Dunlop Masters: 1978.
Ryder Cup: 1975, 1977.

Horton had an unlucky 1982 season as he was plagued by painful tennis elbow, but he remained the 'Mr. Nice Guy' of the circuit and is a likely future Ryder Cup captain. He was controversially overlooked for this event for several years until 1965, when he proved his point by halving with Hale Irwin and beating Lou Graham. One of the most respected teachers, he has helped set up seasonal schools for young professionals. He started playing himself when he was five and captained the juniors at Royal Jersey at 11. He was later coached by Max Faulkner and picked up some of his mannerisms.

Warren Humphreys

Born: April 1, 1952, Kingston, Surrey, England.
Lives: Richmond, Surrey.
Height: 5–10.   *Weight:* 154.
Turned Pro: 1971.
Career Highlights
English Amateur: 1971.
Walker Cup: 1971.

Humphreys has never quite fulfilled the promise he showed as an amateur, although he seemed poised to win his first national title at the end of 1981, when he was involved in a play-off for the South African Open with Gary Player and John Bland. But Player once again pulled it out of the bag for his 13th native Open. Warren's most satisfying amateur memory was being a member of the winning 1971 Walker Cup squad.

Joe Inman

Born: November 29, 1947, Indianapolis, Indiana, U.S.A.
Lives: Clover, South Carolina.
Height: 5–11. *Weight:* 155.
Turned Pro: 1972.
Career Highlights
Walker Cup: 1969.
Kemper Open: 1976.

Inman's best year was 1976, when he won his one tour victory – the Kemper Open – and finished 38th in the money list. His career earnings now top the half million dollar mark. Married to Nancy, with a son Craig.

Hale Irwin

Born: June 3, 1945, Joplin, Missouri, U.S.A.
Lives: Frontenac, Missouri.
Height: 6–0. *Weight:* 170.

Turned Pro: 1968.
Career Highlights
U.S. Open: 1974, 1979.
World Match Play: 1974, 1975.
Ryder Cup: 1975, 1977, 1979, 1981.
World Cup Individual: 1979.
Heritage Classic: 1971, 1973.
Western Open: 1975.
Atlanta Classic: 1975, 1977.
Hawaiian Open: 1979.
Hall of Fame: 1977.

Irwin is one of the game's stylists and also one with the most pride. When he slumped to 38th in the money list in 1980, he started all over again on his swing. He is remarkably consistent, going from early 1975 through to 1978 – 86 tournaments – without missing a 36-hole cut, the third best record in tour history. He has won big tournaments all over the world, including Britain, Australia, South Africa and Japan. He is a graduate of the University of Colorado, where he was a star defensive back. '*Football's easier on the emotions,*' he says. '*You can get rid of them*

Hale Irwin.

57

by tackling someone. In golf the pressures just keep building'. One of his most stunning performances in a career of 13 U.S. tour victories was in the 1977 Hall of Fame Classic at Pinehurst, where he finished with an incredible 20-under par 264. Married to Sally, with two children.

Tony Jacklin

Born: July 7, 1944, Scunthorpe,
  Lincolnshire, England.
Lives: Jersey.
Height: 5–9. *Weight:* 173.
Turned Pro: 1962.
Career Highlights
British Open: 1969.
U.S. Open: 1970.
Dunlop Masters: 1967, 1973.
Jacksonville Open: 1968, 1972.
Italian Open: 1973.
German Open: 1979.
Sun Alliance PGA: 1982.
Ryder Cup 1967, 1969, 1971, 1973,
  1975, 1977, 1979.

Tony Jacklin.

The man who gave British golf its biggest shot in the arm with his Open victory at Lytham in 1969, *'Jacko'* is still the biggest draw for his compatriots. Even now the sight of Jacklin in full cry represents the best iron-striking possible. He has the ability to make the game look so easy and then blow it by erratic putting.

He was Rookie of the Year in 1973 and his biggest triumphs came after he had tested his game in the pressure cooker of the American tour. The first of his two Jacksonville Open victories in 1968 signposted a glorious future. He became the first Briton since Max Faulkner in 1951 to win the Open, topped by a monster drive on Lytham's 18th with no thoughts of safety first, despite a two stroke cushion. He then won the U.S. Open by a mile at Chaska, Minnesota, to become the first British player since Harry Vardon to hold both titles simultaneously and the first to hold the title since Ted Ray in 1920.

He was desperately unlucky in the

British Opens of 1970 and 1972 when the cruelty of the weather and then the unbelievable luck of Lee Trevino would have broken most men. Tax and other problems did cause a decline, but Jacklin is still a winner and in 1982 beat German Bernhard Langer in a play-off for the Sun Alliance British PGA.

Peter Jacobsen

Born: March 4, 1954, Portland, Oregon, U.S.A.
Lives: Portland, Oregon.
Height: 6–3. *Weight:* 190.
Turned Pro: 1976.
Career Highlights
Oregon Open: 1976.
North California Open: 1976.
Western Australian Open: 1979.
Buick-Goodwrench Open: 1980.

Despite a series of illnesses, including an operation on his vocal cords, Jacobsen has steadily climbed up the money list. His other achievements include comic imitations of the other players but he is also in demand at golf clinics. A keen guitarist and all-round musician, Peter is married to Jan, with a daughter Amy.

Barry Jaeckel

Born: February 14, 1949, Los Angeles, California, U.S.A.
Lives: Los Angeles, California.
Height: 5–10½. *Weight:* 160.
Turned Pro: 1971.
Career Highlights
French Open: 1972.
Tallahassee Open: 1978.

Jaeckel took four years to qualify for the tour and has always been erratic. He won the 1978 Tallahassee Open and tied for the 1981 Tournament Players

Peter Jacobsen.

Championship, but lost a three-way play-off to Floyd. He is the son of Richard Jaeckel, a character actor who has appeared in films and television series. Married to Evelyn.

David Jagger

Born: June 9, 1949, Selby, Yorkshire, England.
Lives: Selby.
Height: 6–1. *Weight:* 155.
Turned Pro: 1966.
Career Highlights
Kenyan Open: 1974.
Nigerian Open: 1975, 1982.

Jagger struggles on the European circuit, but makes lucrative raids on the Safari circuit in the winter and claimed the Kalahari Classic and the Nigerian Open in 1982.

Mark James

Born: October 28, 1953, Manchester, Lancashire, England.
Lives: Leeds.
Height: 5–11.   *Weight:* 170.
Turned Pro: 1975.
Career Highlights
English Amateur: 1974.
Sun Alliance Match Play Championship: 1978.
Welsh Classic: 1979.
Carrolls Irish Open: 1979, 1980.
Italian Open: 1982.
Sao Paulo Open: 1981.
Walker Cup: 1975.
Ryder Cup: 1977, 1979, 1981.

After a splendid amateur career when he won the English title in 1974 and was runner up to America's Marvin Giles in the British Amateur the next year, James' professional career has been constantly held up by putting

Mark James.

problems. These were highlighted in the final competition in Britain in 1982, when he three-putted two of the last three greens and took all the pressure off Gordon Brand Jnr. in the Bob Hope Classic. He was one of the early winners of the year, however, as he carried off the Italian Open.

Don January

Born: November 20, 1929, Plainview, Texas, U.S.A.
Lives: Dallas, Texas.
Height: 6–0.   *Weight:* 168.
Turned Pro: 1955.
Career Highlights
PGA Championship: 1967.
Dallas Open: 1956.
Tucson Open: 1960, 1963.
Philadelphia Classic: 1966.
Tournament of Champions: 1968, 1976.
Jacksonville Open: 1970.
Ryder Cup 1965, 1977.

January restricts himself mainly to the lucrative Seniors' circuit, but still creams off substantial sums from the official tour on hit-and-run raids. He had 11 circuit successes, starting with the Dallas Open in 1956 and ending with the MONY Tournament of Champions in 1976. Married to Patricia, with three children.

Tom Jenkins

Born: December 14, 1947, Houston, Texas, U.S.A.
Lives: Alachua, Florida.
Height: 5–11.   *Weight:* 165.
Turned Pro: 1971.
Career Highlight
Philadelphia Classic: 1975.

Jenkins took up golf at 16, when an

injury to his pitching arm ended his baseball hopes. He almost quit the tour in 1980, but returned to form the following year by sharing in a three-way tie in the Wickes-Andy Williams-San Diego Open with Bruce Lietzke and Ray Floyd: Lietzke won with a birdie on the second hole. A keen camper and gardener, Tom is married to Lynn, with a daughter, Melanie.

David Jones
Born: June 22, 1947, Bangor, Northern Ireland.
Lives: Bangor.
Height: 6–5. *Weight:* 175.
Turned Pro: 1968.
Career Highlight
PGA Club Pros' Championship: 1978, 1979.

Jones is one of the last remaining genuine club professionals who make occasional sorties out on to the circuit. He cut down his appearances following six lean years after joining the paid ranks. He has represented the PGA in the mini-Ryder Cup events against America and was captain of the team in 1982.

Grier Jones
Born: May 6, 1946, Wichita, Kansas, U.S.A.
Lives: Wichita, Kansas.
Height: 5–10. *Weight:* 170.
Turned Pro: 1968.
Career Highlights
U.S. NCAA Championship: 1967.
Hawaiian Open: 1972.
Robinson Fall Classic: 1972.
Disney Team Championship: 1977.

Jones was a medallist in the 1968 autumn qualifying school after graduating from Oklahoma State in the

David Jones.

same year. Though named Rookie of the Year in 1969, he has not lived up to his early promise. His first victory was the 1972 Hawaiian Open and he followed with the Robinson Fall Classic in the same season. That year he finished fourth on the money list with 140,000 dollars. His third and last tour victory was the 1977 Disney Team Championship with Gibby Gilbert. Married to Jane, with five children.

Michael King

Born: February 15, 1950, London, England.
Lives: Berkshire.
Height: 6–2.   *Weight:* 182.
Turned Pro: 1974.
Career Highlights
SOS Talisman TPC: 1979.
Walker Cup: 1969, 1973.
Ryder Cup: 1979.

The handsome King maintains his debonair approach although troubled by a persistent back injury. He was a consistent winner on the amateur circuit and played in two Walker Cup events. He won his Ryder Cup cap in 1979 and gained his lone tournament victory – in the Tournament Players' Championship – the week after the match.

Tom Kite

Born: December 9, 1949, Austin, Texas, U.S.A.
Lives: Austin, Texas.
Height: 5–8.   *Weight:* 155.
Turned Pro: 1972.
Career Highlights
European Open: 1980.
Walker Cup: 1971.
IVB-Bicentennial Classic: 1976.
B.C. Open: 1978.

Tom Kite.

Inverrary Classic: 1981.
Ryder Cup: 1979, 1981.

An outstanding amateur, the bespectacled Kite was runner up to Lanny Wadkins in the 1970 U.S. Amateur and shared the 1972 National Collegiate title with Ben Crenshaw. He quickly developed into one of the steadiest players on the tour. In 1973, when named Rookie of the Year, he missed the cut only three times out of 35. In 1981, when he was placed 10th or better in 21 of his 35 starts, he was top money winner, ending Tom Watson's four-year reign.

His first tour success was the IVB-Bicentennial Classic in 1976. He finished third in the 1982 money list but his only victory was Arnold Palmer's Bay Hill Classic in Orlando, an appropriate success by the first recipient of the Palmer Award for being the tour's number one money winner the previous year. Married to Christy, with a daughter, Stephanie.

Bernhard Langer

Born: August 27, 1957, Anhousen, Germany.
Lives: Auchsberg, Germany.
Height: 5–9. *Weight:* 154.
Turned Pro: 1972.
Career Highlights
Dunlop Masters: 1980.
Columbian Open: 1980.
German Open: 1981, 1982.
Bob Hope British Classic: 1981.
Ryder Cup: 1981.

Langer is the best golfer ever produced in Germany and in 1980 he became the first German to win a main tournament. His early career was handicapped by putting problems, but he returned to basics for a phenomenal 1981, topping the European Order of Merit, claiming two tournament victories and finishing second behind Bill Rogers in the British

Open at Sandwich. The putting doubts reappeared in 1982, but he did not disappoint his growing army of home fans when he successfully defended the German Open at Stuttgart, beating Bill Longmuir at the first sudden-death hole.

He became one of the best known golfers on television after his exploits in the 1981 Benson and Hedges, when his ball became lodged in a tree. He climbed into the branches and chipped on to the green, but there was no joy for the modern-day Tarzan as Tom Weiskopf won the tournament by one stroke.

Bernhard Langer.

Bernhard Langer.

Bruce Lietzke

Born: July 18, 1951, Kansas City,
  Kansas, U.S.A.
Lives: Jay, Oklahoma.
Height: 6–2. *Weight:* 185.
Turned Pro: 1974.
Career Highlights
Texas Amateur Champion: 1971.
Tucson Open: 1977, 1979.
Hawaiian Open: 1977.
Bob Hope Classic: 1981.
San Diego Open: 1981.
Byron Nelson Classic: 1981.
Canadian Open: 1978.
Ryder Cup: 1981.

Lietzke stopped playing golf after leaving the University of Houston in 1973
as he was bored with the game. After six
months, however, he resumed and
turned professional. He won his first
tournament – the Joe Garagiola-
Tucson Open – in 1977 and within a
month had claimed the Hawaiian Open

Bruce Lietzke.

Sally Little.

as well. He had three tour victories in
1981, starting with the Bob Hope
Desert Classic. In June 1981 Bruce
became Jerry Pate's brother-in-law by
marrying Pate's wife's sister Rosemarie.
He began golf at the age of five when his
brother Duane, the assistant pro at a
club in Kansas, gave him a set of sawn-
off clubs. At the University of Houston
– where he won the Texas Amateur title
– he roomed with Bill Rogers.

Sally Little

Born: October 12, 1951, Cape Town,
  South Africa.
Lives: Lakeland, Florida, U.S.A.
Height: 5–8. *Weight:* 124.
Turned Pro: 1971.
Career Highlights

South African Champion: 1971.
LPGA Championship: 1980.
Women's International: 1976, 1981.

Sally, who started playing when she was 12, won a string of titles in her native South Africa before joining the U.S. circuit in 1971, when she was named Rookie of the Year. Her breakthrough really came in 1976, however, when she holed a bunker shot on the last to beat Jan Stephenson in the Women's International.

Gene Littler
Born: July 2, 1930, San Diego,
  California, U.S.A.
Lives: Rancho Sante Fe, California.
Height: 5–9. *Weight:* 158.
Turned Pro: 1954.
Career Highlights
U.S. Amateur Champion: 1953.
U.S. Open: 1961.
Canadian Open: 1965.
Tournament of Champions: 1955,
  1956, 1957.
Phoenix Open: 1955, 1959, 1969.
Greensboro Open: 1969.
Bing Crosby Pro-Am 1975.
Westchester Classic 1975.
Houston Open: 1977.
Ryder Cup: 1961, 1963, 1965, 1967,
  1969, 1971, 1975.

'The Gene Machine' possesses a textbook swing which stands up to all weathers and is obviously a consistent money winner. In the spring of 1972, he was told he was suffering from cancer of the lymph glands and that major surgery was essential. Astonishingly he came back, patiently redeveloping a sense of feel in his afflicted arm and, in 1973, claimed his 25th tournament victory in the St. Louis Children's Hospital Classic.

Gene Littler.

He had an outstanding amateur record and chalked up his first tour victory at San Diego as an amateur in 1954. He got the message and turned professional the next week. He concentrates now on the Seniors' tour and his collection of antique cars.

Bill Longmuir
Born: June 10, 1953. Basildon, Essex.
Lives: Basildon.
Height: 6–0. *Weight:* 158.
Turned Pro: 1968.
Career Highlights
Nigerian Open: 1976, 1980.
New Zealand Southland Classic: 1976.

Longmuir lost his chance of two European titles in 1982 when he was beaten in two play-offs in the space of a month. Ian Woosnam pipped him for the Swiss Open and then Bernhard Langer managed to retain his native German Open.

Bill Longmuir.

Longmuir won national prominence when he shot a splendid 65 to lead the first round of the 1979 British Open at Lytham. His outward 29 equalled the championship record. But there was no happy ending as he plummetted down the field and finished 27 strokes behind the winner, Tom Watson. He is a consistent winner on the Safari Circuit.

Mark Lye
Born: November 13, 1952, Vallejo, California, U.S.A.
Lives: Napa, California.
Height: 6–2. *Weight:* 175.
Turned Pro: 1975.
Career Highlights
Topped Australian Order of Merit: 1976.
Australian Champion of Champions: 1976.

Lye twice failed the American Qualify-

ing School so he set off to gain experience and won tournaments in Australia and Switzerland. He passed school in 1976 and cut out overseas trips. He took to golf because he was small as a boy, but in his two years of college at San Jose State he put on almost six inches and sixty pounds.

Sandy Lyle
Born: February 9, 1958, Shrewsbury, Shropshire, England.
Lives: Shropshire.
Height: 6–1. *Weight:* 172.
Turned Pro: 1977.
Career Highlights
English Amateur Stroke Play: 1975, 1977.
British Youths: 1977.
Nigerian Open: 1978.
European Open: 1979.
World Cup Individual: 1980.
Coral Welsh Classic: 1980.

67

Sandy Lyle.

French Open: 1981.
Lawrence Batley International: 1981,
1982.
Walker Cup: 1977.
Ryder Cup: 1979, 1981.

There was never any doubt where
Lyle's future lay. The son of Alex Lyle,
the professional at Hawkstone Park, he
had a golf club in his hand at the same
time as a rattle. He experienced a magnificent amateur career, winning the
English Open Stroke Play Championship twice and in 1975 he represented
England at boy, youth and full international level.

He was Rookie of the Year in 1978
and topped the European money list the
next two seasons. He won the individual trophy for Scotland in the 1980
World Cup and was Britain's second
finalist in the World Match Play
Championship, losing by one hole to
Greg Norman. In 1982 he suffered a
similar disappointment, losing to Sevvy
Ballesteros on the first play-off hole of
the same tournament. He has been less
successful than his great rival Nick
Faldo on his occasional visits to
America, but he could dominate
Europe for years ahead.

In 1981, he married Christine Trew,
a professional golfer and tournament
winner on the WPGA tour.

John Mahaffey

Born: May 9, 1948, Kerrville, Texas,
U.S.A.
Lives: Houston, Texas.
Height: 5–9. *Weight:* 155.
Turned Pro: 1971.
Career Highlights
U.S. PGA Champion: 1978.
Bob Hope Desert Classic: 1979.
Kemper Open: 1980.
Ryder Cup: 1979.

After a breakthrough in the 1978 PGA
Championship, when he beat Tom
Watson and Jerry Pate in a play-off.
Mahaffey's headlong progress was
checked by a series of injuries. Tendon
trouble in his left elbow threatened his
career and this was followed by a
broken finger and torn hand and wrist
tendons when he stubbed a club in a
bunker at Pebble Beach. A keen fisher-
man, he graduated from the University
of Texas with a degree in psychology.
Married to Susie.

John Mahaffey.

69

Roger Maltbie.

Roger Maltbie

Born: June 30, 1951, Modesto,
  California, U.S.A.
Lives: Los Galos, California.
Height: 5–10.   *Weight:* 175.
Turned Pro: 1973,
Career Highlights
California State Open: 1974.
Quad Cities Open: 1975.
Pleasant Valley Classic: 1975.
Magnolia Classic: 1980.
Memorial Tournament: 1976.

After starting his rookie year winning
back-to-back tournaments – the Ed
McMahon-Quad Cities Open and the
Pleasant Valley Classic– Maltbie made
progress over the next two years, but
then sank almost without trace, plum-
meting to 155th in the 1979 money list.
He clawed his way back by hard work
and had three top ten finishes in 1981.
A student of music, Roger is married to
Donna.

Brian Marchbank

Born: April 20, 1958, Perth, Scotland.
Lives: Gleneagles, Scotland.
Height: 5–8.   *Weight:* 147.
Turned Pro: 1979.
Career Highlights
British Boys: 1975.
British Youths': 1978.
Walker Cup: 1979.

Marchbank was born into the game, as
his father Ian is the professional of the
internationally famous Gleneagles
Hotel in Scotland. He is taking time to
make the adjustment to the professional ranks, but finished second to
Greg Norman in the 1982 State Express
Classic.

Graham Marsh

Born: January 14, 1944, Kalgoorie,
  Western Australia.
Lives: Dalkeith, Western Australia.

Height: 5–10. *Weight:* 170.
Turned Pro: 1968.
Career Highlights
World Match Play: 1977.
Swiss Open: 1970, 1972.
Indian Open: 1971, 1973.
German Open: 1972.
Scottish Open: 1973.
Dunlop Masters: 1976.
Benson and Hedges: 1976, 1980.
Lancome Trophy: 1977.
Dutch Open: 1979.

A typical Australian globe-trotter with victories all over the world, Marsh has done particularly well on the lucrative Asian circuit, including three victories in successive weeks in 1975. He was American Rookie of the Year in 1977 when he was 22nd on the money list. He won the World Match Play the same year when he beat Ray Floyd in the final.

His brother is Rod Marsh, the Australian Test cricketer and arguably

Graham Marsh.

the world's best wicket-keeper. Married to Julie, with two children.

Steve Martin

Born: December 21, 1955, Dundee, Scotland.
Lives: Dundee.
Height: 5–10. *Weight:* 155.
Turned Pro: 1977.
Career Highlights
Walker Cup: 1977.
Scottish Open Amateur: 1976.

An outstanding stroke player as an amateur, Martin's victories included the 1976 Scottish Open Amateur, but he is still waiting for his first pro tournament success. He has experience success in team events. He was a member of the victorious Britain and Ireland team in the 1976 Eisenhower Trophy and, with Sandy Lyle, took Scotland into second place in the 1980 World Cup.

Carl Mason

Born: June 25, 1953, Reading, Berkshire, England.
Lives: Reading.
Height: 6–1. *Weight:* 168.
Turned Pro: 1973.
Career Highlights
British Youths': 1973.
Hennessy Cognac Cup: 1980.
World Cup team: 1980.

Mason turned professional after winning the British Youths' Championship and tasted real success in 1980. He was top Briton in the 1980 British Open, when he tied fourth place with Jack Nicklaus and was picked by Britain for the World and Hennessy Cups. Although he failed to win a tournament in 1982, he drove away from the Tournament Players' Championship in style, as he won a £15,000 car for a hole in one.

Jerry McGee

Born: July 21, 1943, New Lexington, Ohio, U.S.A.
Lives: East Palestine, Ohio.
Height: 5–9. *Weight:* 160.
Turned Pro: 1966.
Career Highlights
Ryder Cup: 1977.
Pensacola Open: 1975.
Philadelphia Classic: 1977.
Kemper Open: 1979.
Greater Hartford Open: 1979.

Now director of golf at Oak Tree Country Club, Pennsylvania, McGee makes only limited assaults on the circuit. He achieved his first big victory – the 1975 Pensacola Open – after nine years of trying. Married to Jill, with three children.

Mark McNulty

Born: October 25, 1953, Johannesburg, South Africa.
Lives: Johannesburg.
Height: 5–9. *Weight:* 179.
Turned Pro: 1978.
Career Highlights
Greater Manchester Open: 1979.
German Open: 1980.
Malaysian Open: 1980.

A former South African amateur international, McNulty experienced no difficulty in making the top 60 during his four years on the European circuit. He claimed two tournament victories, including the German Open in 1980, when he also won the Malaysian Open. He was not an admirer of British weather and hankered for the sun on his back. He is now finding the going tough on the United States tour.

Steve Melnyk

Born: February 26, 1947, Brunswick, Georgia, U.S.A.
Lives: Amelia Island, Florida.
Height: 6–2. *Weight:* 220.
Turned Pro: 1971.
Career Highlights
U.S. Amateur: 1969.
British Amateur: 1971.
Walker Cup: 1969, 1971.

Melnyk won virtually everything as an amateur and was the leading amateur in the 1970 British Open and in the U.S. Masters in 1971. But since turning pro he has managed only two placings in the U.S. tour top 60 money earners for a season. He gained a degree in business studies at the University of Florida. Married to Debby, with one son.

Nancy Melton (née Lopez)

Born: January 6, 1957, Torrance, California, U.S.A.
Lives: Palm Coast, Florida.
Height: 5–7. *Weight:* 122.
Turned Pro: 1977.
Career Highlights
Curtis Cup: 1976.
Amateur Cup team: 1976.
LPGA Championship: 1978.
Colgate European Open: 1978, 1979.
Colgate Far East Open: 1978.
Coca-Cola Classic: 1978, 1979.
Women's International: 1979.
Colgate Dinah Shore: 1981.
Just 12 when she won the New Mexico Women's Amateur Championship, Nancy became an unstoppable machine in her second year on the American women's circuit. She won nine tournaments, including five consecutively, to

Nancy Melton.

finish as both Rookie of the Year and Player of the Year. She married sports commentator Tim Melton on her 22nd birthday.

Johnny Miller

Born: April 29, 1947, San Franciso, California, U.S.A.
Lives: Mapleton, Utah.
Height: 6–2. *Weight:* 185.
Turned Pro: 1969.
Career Highlights
U.S. Junior Champion: 1964.
U.S. Open: 1973.
British Open: 1976.
World Cup: 1973.
Heritage Classic: 1972, 1974.
Bing Crosby Pro-Am: 1974.
Phoenix Open: 1974, 1975.
Tucson Open: 1974, 1975, 1981.
Tournament of Champions: 1974.

Westchester Classic: 1974.
Bob Hope Desert Classic: 1976.
Inverrary Classic: 1980.
Los Angeles Open: 1981.
Ryder Cup: 1975, 1981.

An impressive striker of the ball, Miller hit the tournament scene like a tornado and threatened to dominate the tour for years. He claimed 20 worldwide victories between 1971 and 1976 and left his rivals gasping. A final round 63 gave him the U.S. Open in 1973 and he and Jack Nicklaus, not surprisingly, won the World Cup. He picked up eight tour victories the next year after winning the first three events of the season. Miller made a sensational start to 1975, winning the Phoenix Open with a 24-under par score and then the Tucson Open with a 25-under par score. He carded a 61 in each tournament.

Johnny Miller.

Johnny Miller at the British Open 1980.

Then he began to spend more time with his family, his game turned sour and he plunged to 111th in the 1978 money list. Things began to pick up and 1981 saw the real Johnny Miller setting courses on fire. His earnings rose to almost 200,000 dollars in 1981 and he opened 1982 with the biggest individual win on record – 500,000 dollars – in the Million Dollar Sun City Challenge in Bophuthatswana after a nine-hole play-off with Sevvy Ballesteros. Miller is a protegé of Billy Casper and, like Casper, is a strict Mormon. Married to Linda, with six children.

Orville Moody

Born: December 9, 1933, Chicasha, Oklahoma, U.S.A.
Lives: Plano, Texas.
Height: 5–10. *Weight:* 185.
Turned Pro: 1967.
Career Highlights
U.S. Open: 1969.
Hong Kong Open: 1969.
World Series of Golf: 1969.
World Cup Team Title: (with Lee Trevino) 1969.

Part Cherokee Indian, Moody rejected college for the Army and, after a spell as a rifle instructor, was placed in charge of all golf activities. He served in Japan, Korea, Germany and the United States and claimed three Korean Opens as a serviceman.

In 1967 he gave up his 14-year Army career to try the tour for two years: if he failed it would be back to uniform. He almost gave up but eventually kept to his two-year plan and surprised everybody by winning the 1969 U.S. Open at the Champions Club, Houston, ahead of Deane Beman, Al Geiberger and Bob Rosburg. This remains his only American tour victory, but it gives him unlimited exempt status. Married to Beverley, with four children.

Gil Morgan

Born: September 25, 1946, Wewoka, Oklahoma, U.S.A.
Lives: Edmond, Oklahoma.
Height: 5–10. *Weight:* 168.
Turned Pro: 1972.
Career Highlights
All-American Collegiate Winner: 1968.
World Series of Golf: 1978.
B.C. Open: 1977.
Los Angeles Open: 1978.
Memphis Classic: 1979.
Ryder Cup: 1979.

Orville Moody.

Well known as an amateur, Morgan delayed his entry into the professional ranks until he qualified in optometry. A consistent top-ten finisher, with a fluid swing, he had to wait until 1977 before he lifted his first tour victory with a success in the B.C. Open. Two tournament wins the next year – and number two on the money list – did not provide the big lift-off: but he has never been in danger of slipping out of the top 60. Married to Jeanine, with a daughter.

Gil Morgan.

Ian Mosey

Born: August 29, 1951, Manchester, Lancashire, England.
Lives: Manchester.
Height: 5–11. *Weight:* 160.
Turned Pro: 1972.
Career Highlights
Merseyside International: 1980.
Kalahari Classic: 1980.
Holiday Inns, South Africa 1981.

A former English amateur international at boy, youth and full level, Mosey finds it difficult to string four rounds together in the professional school. He is still waiting for a main tournament success although he took the semi-official Merseyside International in 1980 and has won several large cheques in South Africa. He is the son of BBC radio cricket commentator Don Mosey.

Bob Murphy

Born: February 14, 1943, Brooklyn, New York, U.S.A.
Lives: Delray Beach, Florida.
Height: 5–10. *Weight:* 215.
Turned Pro: 1967.
Career Highlights
U.S. Amateur Champion: 1965.
Philadelphia Classic: 1968.
Thunderbird Classic: 1968.
Greater Hartford Open: 1970.
Inverrary Classic: 1975.
Walker Cup: 1967.
Ryder Cup: 1975.

A pick-up game of football changed the course of Murphy's life. He went to the University of Florida on a baseball scholarship as a pitcher, but an injured shoulder in the football match directed him to a third sport – golf. It was love at

Bob Murphy.

Larry Nelson.

first sight: he won everything he tried.

As well as taking the U.S. Amateur crown in 1965, he swept the board in Florida. In his first year on the circuit in 1968 he won the Philadelphia and Thunderbird Classics back-to-back and, not surprisingly, earned the Rookie of the Year title. His career has not remained at those dizzy heights, however, partly because of his poor play-off record: he has lost five out of six. Married to Gail, with a daughter Kimberly.

Ewen Murray
Born: October 7, 1954, Scotland.
Lives: Croydon, Surrey.
Height: 6–0.   *Weight:* 154.
Turned Pro: 1971.
Career Highlights
World Junior: 1971.
Zambian Open: 1980.

A former Scottish amateur international, Murray is yet another golfer to be afflicted with back trouble. He found the whole of the 1982 season hard going and was frequently compelled to use irons off the tee. He won the World Junior title in 1971, the year he turned professional.

Larry Nelson
Born: September 10, 1947, Fort Payne, Alabama, U.S.A.
Lives: Acworth, Georgia.
Height: 5–9.   *Weight:* 150.
Turned Pro: 1971.
Career Highlights
U.S. PGA Championship: 1981.
Inverrary Classic: 1979.
Western Open: 1979.
Atlanta Classic: 1980.
Greensboro Open: 1981.
Ryder Cup: 1979, 1981.

The best is yet to come as Nelson is a man in a hurry. After a normal all-American outlook at school, where he played baseball and basketball, he did two years military service. He then worked for a while at Lockheeds, before being hooked by golf when he went to a driving range in 1969. He became an assistant pro at the Pine Tree Club in Kennesaw, Georgia, and gained his players' card after only four years in the game.

His short career has a curious pattern of one hot season followed by a moderate one: second in the moneylist in 1979, down to 11th in 1980, followed by the Greater Greensboro Open and the P.G.A. Championship in 1981. He enjoys match play and is undefeated in nine consecutive Ryder Cup matches. Married to Gayle, with two sons.

Jack Newton.

ports in his shoes. A real outdoors man who enjoys hunting, fishing and surfing, Jack is married to former promotions girl Jackie, with a son, Clint.

Jack Newton

Born: January 30, 1950, Sydney, Australia.
Lives: Sydney.
Height: 5–10. *Weight:* 190.
Turned Pro: 1971.
Career Highlights
Dutch Open: 1972.
Buick Open: 1978.
Australian Open: 1979.

Newton is a big-hitting, muscular Australian with a good temperament who came close to winning two majors. He lost the 1975 British Open by one stroke in play-off with Tom Watson and finished joint second with Gibby Gilbert behind Sevvy Ballesteros in the 1980 U.S. Masters. Unlucky with injuries, he struggled on the American circuit after qualifying in 1975. An elbow injury took time to heal and an injury to his left foot lasted two years. As a result he must now wear steel sup-

Bobby Nicholls

Born: April 14, 1936, Louisville, Kentucky, U.S.A.
Lives: Naples, Florida.
Height: 6–2. *Weight:* 195.
Turned Pro: 1959.
Career Highlights
U.S. PGA Champion: 1964.
Carling World Open: 1964.
Houston Open: 1962, 1965.
Westchester Classic: 1973.
Canadian Open: 1974.

Nicholls was lucky to live after a car crash when he was 18: he received a broken pelvis, back injuries, brain concussion and internal injuries. Unconscious for two weeks and paralyzed from the waist down, he was detained in hospital for over three months. He received a golf scholarship and two years after playing on the tour he received the Ben Hogan Award for his courage. He has won 12 tour victories, but lost form after playing in the Lee Trevino–Jerry Heard threesome which was hit by bolt lightning during the 1975 Western Open. Married to Nancy, with three children.

Jack Nicklaus

Born: January 21, 1940, Columbus, Ohio, U.S.A.
Lives: North Palm Beach, Florida and Muirfield Village, Ohio.
Height: 5–11. *Weight:* 180.
Turned Pro: 1961.
Career Highlights
U.S. Amateur 1959, 1961.
U.S. Open: 1962, 1967, 1972, 1980.
British Open: 1966, 1970, 1978.

U.S. Masters: 1963, 1971, 1973, 1975, 1980.
U.S. PGA: 1963, 1971, 1973, 1975, 1980.
Australian Open: 1964, 1968, 1971, 1975, 1976, 1978.
World Cup winning teams: 1963, 1964, 1966, 1967, 1971, 1973.
World Series of Golf champion: 1962, 1963, 1967, 1970.
World Match Play: 1970.
Walker Cup: 1959, 1961.
Ryder Cup: 1969, 1971, 1973, 1975, 1977, 1981.

The greatest golfer the world has known: that accolade may have been given first to Harry Vardon, certainly to Bobby Jones, and then through Ben

Jack Nicklaus.

Nicklaus with his wife and son after winning the U.S. Open in 1980.

Hogan and Arnold Palmer to Jack William Nicklaus. And despite the challenge of Tom Watson, the title could stay with the Golden Bear.

After a brilliant amateur career, Nicklaus announced his intentions when he claimed the 1962 U.S. Open as his first victory as a professional, beating Palmer in a play-off. Palmer knew then that his undisputed number one status was under threat. Nicklaus took off into orbit and his magnificent striking, which propelled the ball an enormous distance, gobbled up victories. Only Sam Snead over his 31-year span has claimed more titles.

He has paraded his art all over the world and, in addition to his 17 majors and two U.S. Amateur crowns, he has won the Australian Open six times, been a member of six winning World Cup teams, won the World Series four times and 68 victories on the U.S. tour.

He has 18 international titles and won the 1970 World Match Play Championship when he beat Trevino. There are signs that his reign is over. The zoom lens of television reveals the tortured concentration on the putting green and makes the thousands of 'Jack's Pack' want to hold their breath and close their eyes. His contribution to the game has been enormous both as an ambassador and a golfer.

His record three million dollars in winnings represents only the tip of his fortune. Since parting from Mark McCormack, he has set up Golden Bear Inc. – a highly-diversified conglomerate of 25 companies. One estimate of his income in 1982 put his annual gross revenue in the region of 300 million dollars. His favourite commercial activity is designing golf courses, but the modest Nicklaus still puts his family first, golf second and business third. Married to Barbara, with five children.

Greg Norman

Born: February 10, 1955, Melbourne, Australia.
Lives: Florida, U.S.A.
Height: 6–1.   *Weight:* 185.
Turned Pro: 1976.
Career Highlights
Dunlop Masters: 1981, 1982.
French Open: 1980.
Martini International: 1977, 1979, 1981.
Australian Open: 1980.
Hong Kong Open: 1981.
World Match Play: 1981.
Australian Masters: 1981.
State Express Classic: 1982.
Benson and Hedges: 1982.

The greatest Australian hope since Peter Thomson, Norman intends to tackle the American circuit. He is already based in Florida and is keen to build on his fourth place in the 1981 Masters and joint fifth in the 1982 PGA. Because of his blond hair and big

Greg Norman.

Greg Norman.

hitting – his average length in 1982 was 281 yards – he is known as the 'Great White Shark.' And he has devoured numerous rivals, despite his international schedule.

He claimed three victories on the 1982 European tour, winning the State Express Classic, the Benson and Hedges International and retaining the Dunlop Masters by a vast margin. He also encouraged hackers everywhere when he took a horrific 14 on the par four 17th at Lindrick in the 1982 Martini. He was briefly involved romantically with British tennis star Sue Barker.

Andy North
Born: March 9, 1950, Thorp, Wisconsin, U.S.A.
Lives: Madison, Wisconsin.
Height: 6–4. *Weight:* 215.

Turned Pro: 1972.
Career Highlights
U.S. Open: 1978.
Westchester Classic: 1977.
World Cup Team: 1978.

Impressively-built North lived dangerously when winning the 1978 U.S. Open, his only major so far. He led by two strokes after blowing a comfortable lead, but he still had the cushion of knowing that a bogey at the last would win him the title at Cherry Hills. As it was he needed all five shots after bunkering his third. That Open triumph has not signalled a take-over by him and he was out of the top 60 two years later. Better things seem on the horizon as he admits he is now working harder at his game. Andy's father was a low-handicap player, but another love at school was basketball, where his height helped him gain all-State representative honours. Married to Susan, with two daughters.

Christy O'Connor

Born: December 21, 1924, Galway, Ireland.
Lives: Dublin, Ireland.
Height: 5–10.   *Weight:* 189.
Turned Pro: 1946.
Career Highlights
Dunlop Masters: 1956, 1959.
PGA Match Play: 1957.
Carrolls: 1964, 1966, 1967, 1972.
John Player Classic: 1970.
Ryder Cup: 1955, 1957, 1959, 1961, 1963, 1965, 1967, 1969, 1971, 1973.

O'Connor is one of the greatest tournament professionals produced by Ireland and a big cheque winner. He picked up the first £1,000 prize offered in Britain in 1955 and later won

Andy North.

£25,000 – then far and away the largest prize put up in Europe – by taking the John Player Classic at Hollinwell in 1970. Because of his boyhood in Galway, he was in a class of his own in foul weather and was probably the best user of a driver off the fairway in the world.

He still makes occasional appearances but mainly confines himself to Senior events. He was World Senior Champion in 1976 and 1977 and won the British Seniors for the fifth time in 1982 at the fifth extra hole. He represented Britain and Ireland ten times in the Ryder Cup. His best performances during his long career in the British Open were both at Lytham. He was second behind Peter Thomson in 1965 and joint third in 1961. He was never a consistent putter otherwise he would have ranked alongside the best like Nicklaus, Palmer and Player.

Christy O'Connor Jnr.

Born: August 19, 1948, Galway, Ireland.
Lives: Dublin, Ireland.
Height: 5–11.   *Weight:* 170.
Turned Pro: 1965.
Career Highlights
Zambian Open: 1974.
Carrolls Irish Open: 1975.
Martini International: 1975.
Irish Match Play: 1975.
Ryder Cup: 1975.

He is the nephew of the other Christy O'Connor, but is unable to reproduce the same magical feats and has fallen out of Europe's top 60. He represented Ireland three times in the World Cup, once in partnership with his uncle in 1975. He showed signs of a return to form in the 1982 German Open, when he finished one stroke behind Bernhard Langer and Bill Longmuir.

John O'Leary

Born: August 19, 1949, Dublin, Ireland.
Lives: Dublin.
Height: 6–2. *Weight:* 200.
Turned Pro: 1970.
Career Highlights
Greater Manchester Open: 1976.
Carrolls Irish Open: 1982.
Ryder Cup: 1975.

The colourful O'Leary should be heading for a golden future now that he has finally exorcised his fatal last green slip-up in the 1978 Irish Open. He three-putted from just off the green in front of his own supporters who were already celebrating his victory. His form slumped until he put matters right in Dublin in 1982, holding on to win the Irish Open this time. He has problems with a back injury.

Mark O'Meara

Born: January 13, 1957, Goldsbrough, North Carolina, U.S.A.
Lives: Laguna Niguel, California.
Height: 6–0. *Weight:* 175.
Turned Pro: 1980.
Career Highlight
U.S. Amateur: 1979.

O'Meara had a brilliant amateur career followed by an impressive first year on the tour in 1981 and received the Rookie of the Year award. In addition to winning the 1979 U.S. Amateur, he also picked up the California State Amateur and the Mexican Amateur in the same year. He tied with Dave Eichelberger and Bob Murphy in the 1981 Tallahassee Open, but lost the play-off to Eichelberger. An all-round sportsman who skiis and plays racket-ball, Mark is married to Alicia.

Peter Oosterhuis

Born: May 3, 1948, London, England.
Lives: Santa Barbara, California.
Height: 6–5. *Weight:* 210.
Turned Pro: 1968.
Career Highlights
French Open: 1973, 1974.
Italian Open: 1974.
Canadian Open: 1981.
Walker Cup: 1967.
Ryder Cup: 1971, 1973, 1977, 1979, 1981.

The longest-standing British campaigner on the American circuit, Oosterhuis is now happily settled in California. He played in the Walker Cup while still a schoolboy and his long, lanky frame soon dominated the European tour. After topping their Order of Merit for four successive years, he struck out for the United States. '*If I was to improve my golf, it was the natural thing to do,*' he said.

His conviction had obviously been strengthened by his third position in the 1973 U.S. Masters – the best ever by a British player. His long struggle was rewarded by victory in the 1981 Canadian Open when he received the congratulations of most of the tour regulars. A confidence born of that victory was obvious in 1982, when he won the Spalding Invitational at Pebble Beach, collecting £18,000.

He only makes occasional trips to his home country but has four times been the leading British player in their Open: second in 1974 and 1982, seventh in 1975 and eighth in 1978. Peter's name is Dutch in origin. His father came from Holland to England during World War II and met his wife-to-be. Peter attended Dulwich College in London. He is married to Anne, with sons Robert and Richard.

Peter Oosterhuis.

Simon Owen.

Simon Owen

Born: December 10, 1950,
Christchurch, New Zealand.
Lives: Christchurch.
Height: 6–1. *Weight:* 165.
Turned Pro: 1971.
Career Highlights
German Open: 1974.
New Zealand Open: 1976.

Owen is a World Cup player from New
Zealand who has come extremely close
to lifting two of golf's most prestigious
events. In the 1978 British Open, he led
the winner Jack Nicklaus by one stroke
with three holes to go. But pressure
seemed to get to him and he finished in a
four-way tie for second place. Then he
lost in the final of the World Match Play
to Isao Aoki three and two in the same
year.

Arnold Palmer

Born: September 10, 1929, Latrobe,
Pennsylvania, U.S.A.
Lives: Latrobe, Pennsylvania.

Height: 5–10 *Weight: 180.*
Turned Pro: 1954.
Career Highlights
U.S. Amateur: 1954.
U.S. Open: 1960.
British Open: 1961, 1962.
U.S. Masters: 1958, 1960, 1962, 1964.
World Match Play: 1964, 1967.
Canadian Open: 1955.
Tournament of Champions: 1962,
1965, 1966.
Ryder Cup: 1961, 1963, 1965, 1967,
1971, 1973. Non-Playing captain
1975.
World Cup individual 1967; winning
team: 1960, 1962, 1963, 1964, 1966,
1967.

The game's first folk-hero. More than
anyone, he thrust golf into the multi-
million dollar bracket. The hitching-up
of his trousers, the slow drawl and the
smile spreading into a grin which lit up
his whole face became his trade marks
and guaranteed the success of any tournament.

He was light years removed from the
cool, clinical efficiency of Ben Hogan.
He played golf the way every hacker the
world over would like to play – and
only managed in their dreams. It is
obvious that his attachment to the game
is a love affair that will end only with
death. He is one of the few professional
sportsmen not afraid of showing he
actually enjoys going about his business.

He attacked the course like a human
opponent and 'The Palmer Charge'
became an emotive phrase in the language. One of his classic charges was in
the 1960 U.S. Open at Cherry Hills,
when he started the last round in 15th
place seven strokes behind Mike
Souchak. He birdied six of the first
seven holes for a 65 and winning 280
total.

Arnold Palmer.

Arnold Palmer.

The crowds loved it and 'Arnie's Army' yelled their glee. There seemed a chance that spectators would be split into two sections – the Palmer legions and the rest. Palmer's innate good manners and etiquette helped keep things in order.

Not only did the Palmer boom boost the U.S. circuit but he gave a transfusion to the British Open. His decision to compete in the 1960 Centenary Championship at St. Andrews guaranteed the event would remain one of the four majors. Australian Kel Nagle ruined the party by winning by one stroke, but Palmer returned and won the next two years at Royal Birkdale and Troon. Just as important for the Royal and Ancient was that Palmer's decision to place the Open in the top four events persuaded the rest of the American tour to trek across the Atlantic. No wonder the R & A made him an honorary member in 1979.

He was the first player to reach the million dollar mark in winnings and his fellow professionals owe him a debt too. Under the guidance of Mark McCormack, he converted his popularity into dollars and lit the way ahead. The decision of the Tournament Players' Association to present 'The Arnold Palmer Award' to the tour's leading money winner was a popular one. Tom Kite was the first recipient in 1981.

Obviously the senior events claim a lot of his attention but his few appearances in the big events remain special occasions. When he was up with the leaders after the first round of the 1982 British Open, the overseas division of his army celebrated long into the night. Married to Winifred, Arnie has two daughters, Margaret and Amy.

Sandra Palmer

Born: March 10, 1941, Fort Worth, Texas, U.S.A.
Lives: Boca Raton, Florida.
Height: 5–1½. *Weight:* 117.
Turned Pro: 1964.

Career Highlights
U.S. Open: 1975.
Heritage Open: 1971.
Colgate Dinah Shore: 1975.
Women's International: 1977.
Japan Women's Open: 1970.

Sandra turned pro after working as a caddie on her local golf course. It took her seven years to record her first U.S. tour win but she has gone on to become one of the most consistent money earners in the game, despite her small stature.

Catherine Panton
Born: June 14, 1955, Stirlingshire, Scotland.
Lives: West Finchley, London.
Height: 5–6. *Weight:* 140.
Turned Pro: 1978.

Sandra Palmer.

Career Highlights
Scottish Girls': 1969.
British Champion: 1976.

Catherine is in the top trio of Europe's fledgling women's professional circuit. Despite an outstanding amateur career, she graduated from Edinburgh University before contemplating the tour. She is the daughter of Ryder Cupper, John Panton, one of Scotland's all-time greats.

Jerry Pate
Born: September 16, 1953, Macon, Georgia, U.S.A.
Lives: Pensacola, Florida.
Height: 6–0. *Weight:* 160.
Turned Pro: 1975.
Career Highlights
U.S. Amateur: 1974.
U.S. Open: 1976.
Canadian Open: 1976.
Phoenix Open: 1977.
Southern Open: 1977, 1978.
Memphis Classic: 1981.
Pensacola Open: 1981.
Walker Cup: 1975.
Ryder Cup: 1981.

Pate is a young man in a hurry and the youngest player to make one million dollars on the American tour. He had a brilliant amateur record. He picked up the Florida Amateur championship the same year as the U.S. Amateur and helped the United States win the 1974 World Amateur Team Championship and the 1975 Walker Cup.

He burst onto the tour in 1976 with two national Opens and his $153,000 is the most won by a rookie. Seldom out of the money but, when he won the Danny Thomas-Memphis Classic in 1981 after two years without a first place, he strolled across to the greenside

Jerry Pate.

lake and dived in. He made a big splash again in 1982 when he swam 20 lengths at the Pensacola Junior College to raise money. Married to Soozi, with two children.

Calvin Peete

Born: July 18, 1943, Detroit, Michigan, U.S.A.
Lives: Fort Myers, Florida.
Height: 5–10. *Weight:* 160.
Turned Pro: 1971.
Career Highlights
Greater Milwaukee Open: 1979, 1982.
Anheuser-Busch Classic: 1982.

One of the straightest drivers in the business, the black Peete really established himself in 1982 when he won the Greater Milwaukee Open and Anheuser-Busch Classic in the space of three weeks. This was great tribute to his

character as his early life was a struggle: he was one of 19 children brought up on a farm in one of Florida's poorer areas and had to leave school early to help support the family. He started selling goods to migrant workers, packing his station wagon with merchandise and then driving thousands of miles to find customers. Eventually friends in New York persuaded him to try golf for relaxation in 1966. When he heard of the money on the tour, he was hooked. He claims a fall from a tree at the age of 12 which broke his elbow in three places has aided his accuracy. He is unable to straighten his left arm and says: *'Because of the weakness, I can't get too quick.'* Married to Christine, with four children.

Manuel Pinero

Born: September 1, 1952, Puebla de la

Calzada, Spain.
Lives: Madrid.
Height: 5–7.   *Weight:* 148.
Turned Pro: 1968.
Career Highlights
Swiss Open: 1976, 1981.
Penfold PGA Championship: 1977.
European Open: 1982.
World Cup: 1974, 1976 (winning team), 1978, 1979, 1980.
Ryder Cup: 1981.

Pinero has made steady progress since joining the European circuit in 1972, except for a temporary recession in 1979 which cost him a Ryder Cup place when the team was expanded to include all Europeans. He put that right two years later, climbing into fifth place on the money list and winning his singles against Jerry Pate. His first 1982 victory resulted from a furious charge over the last nine holes for a record 63 to win the European Open at Sunningdale.

Gary Player

Born: November 1, 1935, Johannesburg, South Africa.
Lives: Johannesburg.
Height: 5–7.   *Weight:* 150.
Turned Pro: 1953.
Career Highlights
U.S. Open: 1965.
U.S. Masters: 1961, 1974, 1978.
U.S. PGA: 1962, 1972.
British Open: 1959, 1968, 1974.
World Match Play: 1965, 1966, 1968, 1971, 1973.
World Series; 1965, 1968, 1972.
World Cup: individual winner 1965, 1977.
Tournament of Champions: 1969, 1978.

Manuel Pinero.

Gary Player.

One of the all-time greats and the third man in history to win all four majors, player was placed on the same level with Arnold Palmer and Jack Nicklaus when the 'Big Three' were the box-office stars of the 60's and early 70's. If he had attacked the U.S. tour from a permanent base, he would probably have rewritten the record book. But he kept his roots firmly in South Africa where he virtually claimed permanent possession of every big event, including 13 victories of the South African Open.

He has won more than 120 tournaments all over the world and hit an amazing peak in 1974. In addition to claiming two of the majors, he recorded his 100th victory as a professional and carded a 59 in the second round of the 1974 Brazilian Open. A born fighter, he achieved a fantastic recovery against Tony Lema in the 1965 World Match Play Championship after being seven down with 17 to play. And when he won three-in-a-row in 1978, he was seven strokes behind in the U.S. Masters, seven behind again at the Tournament of Champions and then a mere three behind in the Houston Open. When he won the U.S. Open in 1965, it was the first victory by an overseas player for 45 years. His record of success in all five continents is a tribute to his punishing physical fitness programme that allows him to overcome fatigue and jet lag. Although he is showing increasing interest in his farm, and especially his horses, he promises to be around at the majors for a long time yet. Married to Vivienne with six children, including Wayne who is a promising young pro following father's footsteps.

Gary Player.

Dan Pohl

Born: April 1, 1955, Mount Pleasant, Michigan, U.S.A.
Lives: Mount Pleasant.
Height: 6–0. *Weight:* 180.
Turned Pro: 1977.
Career Highlights
Michigan Amateur: 1975, 1977.
U.S. PGA: third 1981.
Tucson Open: fourth 1981.

Pohl possesses frightening power off the tee, but not always the necessary control. His longest measured drive to date is 359 yards at Abilene, Texas. He earned his tour card at the second attempt, lost it after earning only about 1,000 dollars, but soon regained it. His third place in the 1981 U.S. PGA was an indication of his very steady improvement.

Eddie Polland

Born: June 10, 1947, Newcastle,
  County Down, Northern Ireland.
Lives: Malaga, Spain.
Height: 5–11. *Weight:* 160.
Turned Pro: 1967.
Career Highlights
Sun Alliance Match-Play: 1975.
Spanish Open 1976. 1980.
Ryder Cup 1973.

Injury has frequently upset the Ulster-
man when he has seemed in line to
establish himself. He has made occasional hit-and-run raids on the top
honours, but has lacked consistency.

Eddie Pollard.

Don Pooley

Born: August 27, 1951, Phoenix,
  Arizona, U.S.A.
Lives: Tucson, Arizona.
Height: 6–2. *Weight:* 180.
Turned Pro: 1973.
Career Highlight
B.C. Open: 1980.

Pooley is a determined competitor, who
has really worked to get near the top.
He played the mini-tours after college
and needed three attempts to gain his
card, but lost it after winning only
2,000 dollars in 1976. He regained his
card after going back to school and,

Don Pooley.

Sandra Post.

with a new stance and putting style, gradually began to climb up the ratings. He was given his first set of clubs at the age of seven, was No 1 man at his high school and best player at the University of Arizona. Married to Margaret, with a daughter, Lynn.

Sandra Post

Born: June 4, 1948, Ontario, Canada.
Lives: Boynton Beach, Florida, U.S.A.
Height: 5–4. *Weight:* 120.
Turned Pro: 1968.
Career Highlights
LPGA Championship: 1968.
Colgate Dinah Shore: 1978, 1979.
Colgate Far East Open: 1974.

Sandra won the Canadian junior championship three times after taking up the game at the age of five. At 19 she won the U.S. LPGA championship beating the great Kathy Whitworth in a play-off. Sandra was not to win again for ten years, but in 1979 she was voted Canada's Outstanding Athlete after her second Colgate Dinah Shore success.

Greg Powers
Born: March 17, 1946, Albany, New
  York, U.S.A.
Lives: Tallahassee, Florida.
Height: 6–0. *Weight:* 198.
Turned Pro: 1970.
Career Highlights
Tennessee PGA: 1975, 1977.
Tennessee Open: 1975.
Sun City Open: 1973.

Powers graduated from the 1971
Autumn tour along with Tom Watson,
David Graham, John Mahaffey and
Lanny Wadkins, but is still struggling to
establish himself. He dropped out for
three years to become a club professional in Nashville, but he is back on
tour now and intends to stay.

Martin Poxon
Born: May 27, 1955, Tamworth,
  Staffordshire, England.
Lives: Staffordshire.
Height: 6–0. *Weight:* 168.
Turned Pro: 1976.
Career Highlights
French Junior Match Play: 1974.
Walker Cup: 1975.

He is still failing to fulfill the potential
revealed during his amateur career and
did not make the European top 60 until
his fifth year, when he crept in at 59th.
Despite not having to pre-qualify in
1982, the powerfully built Poxon is still
waiting for his breakthrough.

Nick Price
Born: January 28, 1957, Zimbabwe.
Lives: Johannesburg.
Height: 6–0. *Weight:* 158.
Turned Pro: 1978.
Career Highlights
World Junior Title: 1974.

Nick Price.

Swiss Open: 1980.
South African Masters: 1981.

Price hopes not to be remembered as the
man who threw away the 1982 British
Open at Troon, just as American Doug
Sanders missed a three-and-a-half feet
putt on St. Andrews 18th green in 1970
and then lost to Jack Nicklaus in the
play-off. A double bogey at the 15th
and then a bogey at the 17th saw the
coveted prize slip away and leave Tom
Watson a winner by one stroke. Price
tied for second with Peter Oosterhuis.
Price displayed remarkable resilience
and claimed that it was no disgrace to
finish second. He intends to play in the
United States.

Tom Purtzer
Born: December 5, 1951, Des Moines,
  Iowa, U.S.A.

Lives: Phoenix, Arizona.
Height: 6–0.   *Weight:* 174.
Turned Pro: 1973.
Career Highlights
Glen Campbell Los Angeles Open:
  1977.
Arizona Amateur: 1972.
Southwest Open: 1972.

It is a mystery why Purtzer has not made a bigger impression. He is one of the biggest hitters on the tour and has also discovered consistency, but he has failed to add to his one tour success in 1977. He tied for fourth place in the 1982 British Open two strokes behind Tom Watson. Married to Jacqueline, with a daughter, Laura.

Ronan Rafferty

Born: January 13, 1964, Warrenpoint,
  Northern Ireland.
Lives: Northern Ireland.
Height: 6–0.   *Weight:* 185.
Turned Pro: 1981.

Career Highlights
British Boys': 1979.
Walker Cup: 1981.

Rafferty was rated the best prospect for a decade when he became the youngest person to ever play in the Walker Cup. But he found it hard to get to grips with the professional game and failed in the autumn qualifying school. He played in South Africa and finished 30th in their Order of Merit, gaining exemption for the 1982 European tour.

Judy Rankin

Born: February 18, 1945, St Louis,
  Missouri, U.S.A.
Lives: Midland, Texas.
Height: 5–3.   *Weight:* 110.
Turned Pro: 1962.
Career Highlights
Colgate Dinah Shore: 1976.
Colgate European Open: 1974, 1977.
Colgate Hong Kong Open: 1976.
Peter Jackson Classic: 1977.

Judy Rankin.

The youngest player to win the Missouri Amateur at the age of 14, Judy has gone on to land almost 30 victories on the U.S. women's pro tour. She started playing at the age of six with the tuition of her father. In 1976 she became the first woman player to win more than 100,000 dollars in a season. She has been troubled by back problems in recent seasons.

Noel Ratcliffe

Born: January 17, 1945, Sydney, Australia.
Lives: Sydney.
Height: 6–1. *Weight:* 155.
Turned Pro: 1974.
Career Highlights
Belgian Open: 1978.
South Australian Open: 1977.

Ratcliffe represented Australia as an amateur in the 1972 Eisenhower Trophy and, after victories in Australia and New Guinea, tilted at the European Circuit. Although he won the Belgian Open in 1978, he has found it difficult.

Mike Reid

Born: July 1, 1954, Bainbridge, Maryland, U.S.A.
Lives: Provo, Utah.
Height: 6–0. *Weight:* 154.
Turned Pro: 1976.
Career Highlights
Pacific Coast Amateur: 1976.
World Cup: 1980.

Reid is one of the most accurate drivers on the U.S. tour but is still waiting for his first victory. The closest he has come was the 1978 Pensacola Open when he lost to Mac McLendon in a play-off. He took up golf because his father's career as an Air Force officer meant Mike was

constantly moving home and made him a loner. He was the best scoring amateur in the 1976 U.S. Open, the year he turned pro. His brother is a club pro in Seattle. Married to Randolyn, with a daughter Brendalyn.

Jack Renner

Born: July 6, 1956, Palm Springs, California, U.S.A.
Lives: San Diego, California.
Height: 6–0. *Weight:* 160.
Turned Pro: 1976.
Career Highlights
Manufacturers Hanover-Westchester Classic: 1979.
Pleasant Valley-Jimmy Fund Classic: 1981.
World Junior: 1972.
U.S. Junior: 1973.

Pencil-slim Renner is easy to spot as he wears a similar white cap to the one donned by Ben Hogan for years. His immaculate short game is another connection with the former maestro. His brilliant amateur promise is yet to fully blossom on the circuit. He comes from a golfing family – sister Jane has been on the women's circuit for six years and his brother Jim is also a professional.

Chi Chi Rodriguez

Born: October 23, 1935, Rio Pedras, Puerto Rico.
Lives: Dorado Beach, Puerto Rico.
Height: 5–7. *Weight:* 130.
Turned Pro: 1960.
Career Highlights
Denver: 1963.
Lucky International: 1964.
Western Open: 1964.
Texas Open: 1967.
Greensboro: 1973.
Tallahassee Open: 1979.

Rodriguez was a double tournament winner in 1964, claiming the Lucky International and the Western. For a small man, he hits a tremendous length. He is one of the tour's jesters, but more serious off the course and works hard for charities for deprived children. Christened 'Juan', he came up the hard way as a caddie in Puerto Rico. Not the most elegant of players but his great touch gets him out of all sorts of trouble. Married to Iwalani, with one daughter.

Bill Rogers

Born: September 10, 1951, Waco, Texas, U.S.A.
Lives: Texarkana, Texas.
Height: 6–0.   *Weight:* 150.
Turned Pro: 1974.
Career Highlights
British Open: 1981.
World Series: 1981.
World Match Play: 1979.
Bob Hope Desert Classic: 1978.
Heritage Classic: 1981.
Texas Open: 1981.

Bill Rogers.

Walker Cup: 1973.
Ryder Cup: 1981.

Although the tall Texan had won the Bob Hope Desert Classic in 1978, there were doubters who were labelling him a one-tournament winner despite his consistency and high finishes. In 1979 they found more evidence of their claim when Rogers won 250,500 dollars without a victory. He broke the spell at the back end of the season when he was a surprise winner of the World Match Play, beating Japan's Isao Aoki by one hole.

He was 23rd in the 1980 money list, but took off in 1981 and collected seven titles around the world, of which the British Open was the gem. He hit a straight up and down 72 during the first day's bad conditions, and then went on to beat Germany's Bernhard Langer by four strokes. His father was a lieutenant colonel in the U.S. Air Force and as a young child Bill lived in Germany and Morocco. Married to Beth.

Bill Rogers.

Vivien Saunders

Born: November 24, 1946. Sutton, Surrey, England.
Lives: Oxshott, Surrey.
Height: 5–5. *Weight:* 140.
Turned Pro: 1969.
Career Highlights
British Women's Open: 1977.
Curtis Cup: 1968.

Vivien developed from a tempestuous club-throwing girl international into a pioneer of British Women's Professional Golf. She was the first European to qualify to play on the American women's tour in 1969 but won her first two titles in Australia. She was founder and first chairperson of the British Women's Professional Golf Association, but now makes only occasional playing appearances. She has three University degrees and is a practising solicitor. She concentrates principally on teaching and has written three instruction books.

Bob Shearer

Born: May 28, 1948, Melbourne, Australia.
Lives: Melbourne and North Myrtle Beach, South Carolina, U.S.A.
Height: 6–0. *Weight:* 180.
Turned Pro: 1970.
Career Highlights
Australian Amateur: 1969.
New Zealand Open: 1978.
Madrid Open: 1975.
Tallahassee Open: 1982.

Shearer plays all over the world but concentrated on the American circuit after gaining his card in 1976 and was in the top 60 in 1977 and 1978. He arrested a temporary decline when he started 1982 with a bang. Over four weeks he won the Tallahassee Open,

Viv Saunders.

lost the Michelob-Houston Open in a play-off, tied for second in the U.S.F. & G. and tied for sixth in the Byron Nelson Classic. Married to Kathy, with a son Bobby.

Jim Simons

Born: May 15, 1950, Pittsburg, Pennsylvania, U.S.A.
Lives: Tequesta, Florida.
Height: 5–10. *Weight:* 166.
Turned Pro: 1972.
Career Highlights
First News NBC New Orleans Open: 1977.
Memorial Tournament: 1978.
Walker Cup: 1971.

Many experts still expect Simons to take the tour apart one day, but he has yet to display the consistency he had as an amateur. He had to wait almost five years for his initial tour victory, after losing much of one season with shoulder trouble. After making the 1971 Walker Cup team, he stayed on for the British Amateur at Carnoustie, and lost in the final to team-mate Steve Milnyk. He led the 1971 U.S. Open at Merion after three rounds and finished fifth. He was the low amateur in the following year's Open at Pebble Beach and then took the hint and turned pro. A student of the stock market as well as a fine water-skier, Jim is married to Sherry, with two children.

Scott Simpson

Born: September 17, 1955, San Diego, California, U.S.A.
Lives: San Diego.
Height: 6–2. *Weight:* 178.
Turned Pro: 1977.
Career Highlights
Western Open: 1980.

Scott Simpson.

Walker Cup: 1977.

Simpson started playing when he was only nine years old and impressively climbed the amateur tree winning the National Collegiate titles in 1976 and 1977 for the University of Southern California. That convinced him to turn pro. He topped the 100,000 dollars in 1980, 1981 and 1982. He keeps his powerful build in shape by jogging. Married to Cheryl.

Jenny Lee Smith

Born: December 2, 1948, Newcastle-on-Tyne, Northumberland, England.
Lives: Newcastle-on-Tyne.
Height: 5–5. *Weight:* 140.
Turned Pro: 1977.
Career Highlights
British Open Stroke Play: 1976.

Wills Match Play: 1974.
Curtis Cup: 1974, 1976.

The former hairdresser qualified to play on the American tour during her first year as a professional. She absolutely dominates the British scene being number one money winner in 1981 and 1982.

Des Smyth

Born: February 12, 1952, Drogheda, Northern Ireland.
Lives: Drogheda.

Jenny Lee Smith.

Height: 5–10. *Weight:* 147.
Turned Pro: 1973.
Career Highlights
Sun Alliance Match Play: 1979.
Greater Manchester Open: 1980.
Coral Welsh Classic: 1981.
Ryder Cup: 1979, 1981.

Smyth is the most improved professional on the European circuit, although he failed to win a tournament in 1982. The closest he came was when he lost the play-off to Bernard Gallacher for the Jersey Open. He had a remarkable scoring spell in 1980, when

Des Smyth.

he won the Greater Manchester Open and two lesser tournaments in a three week period, and was 47 under par for the 12 rounds. He is the longest holder of the British PGA Match-Play Championship as the event was discontinued after his victory at York in 1979.

J.C. (Jesse) Snead
Born: October 14, 1941, Hot Springs, Virginia, U.S.A.
Lives: Hot Springs, Virginia and Ponte Vedra Beach, Florida.
Height: 6–2. *Weight:* 190.
Turned Pro: 1964.
Career Highlights
Doral Eastern: 1971.
Tucson Open: 1971.
Philadelphia Open: 1972.
San Diego Open: 1975, 1976.
Southern Open: 1981.
Australia Open: 1973.
Ryder Cup: 1971, 1973, 1975.

Nephew of the legendary Sam Snead, J.C. took a long time to start on the circuit. He needed four years to earn his card but took off after his first two victories at Tucson and Doral during three weeks in 1971 and is now a consistent 100,000 dollar winner. He tied with Dave Stockton for second place in the 1978 U.S. Open and was runner up in the 1973 Masters. One of the game's most colourful characters and a great story teller when in the mood, Snead was a fine all-round athlete as a boy and considered a career in baseball. Married to Sue, with a son, Jason.

Ed Sneed
Born: August 6, 1944, Roanoke, Virginia, U.S.A.
Lives: Pompano Beach, Florida.
Height: 6–2. *Weight:* 190.
Turned Pro: 1967.
Career Highlights

J.C. Snead.

Kaiser Open: 1973.
Greater Milwaukee Open: 1974.
Tallahassee Open: 1977.

Sneed gained his card at the 1968 autumn school and achieved three tournament victories, starting with the Kaiser International Open in 1973. An expert at the more intellectual pursuits of chess and bridge, Ed is a graduate in marketing from Ohio State University. Married to Nancy, with two daughters.

Hollis Stacy

Born: March 16, 1954, Savannah, Georgia, U.S.A.
Lives: Hilton Head, South Carolina.
Height: 5–5. *Weight:* 136.
Turned Pro: 1974.
Career Highlights
U.S. Open: 1977, 1978.
Lady Tara Classic: 1977.
Rail Charity Classic: 1977.

Mayflower Classic: 1979.
Women's International: 1980.
West Virginia Classic: 1981.

Hollis comes from a real golfing family and won the U.S. Junior title three years in a row from 1969–1971. But she had to wait three seasons after joining the U.S. pro tour for her first win. That came in sensational style in the Rail Charity Classic when she smashed the tour record with 271 for the 72 holes. Within a couple of months she had added the U.S. title as well, a championship she retained the following year – only the fourth woman to do so.

Craig Stadler

Born: June 2, 1953, San Diego, California, U.S.A.
Lives: Lake Tahoe, Nevada.
Height: 5–10. *Weight:* 200.
Turned Pro: 1975.

Hollis Stacy.

Craig Stadler.

Career Highlights
U.S. Masters: 1982.
World Series: 1982.
World Junior: 1971.
Bob Hope Desert Classic: 1980.
Greensboro Open: 1980.
Kemper Open: 1981, 1982.
Tucson Open: 1982.
U.S. Amateur: 1973.
Walker Cup: 1975.

Stadler is now showing the confidence he displayed as an amateur and, helped by his play-off victory in the Masters, he topped the 1982 money list. Despite an excellent amateur record, including being national champion in 1973, he failed the first qualifying school. After passing in the spring of 1976, he looked completely lost.

It was not until 1980 when he won two tournaments and finished eighth in the money that he became established. He finished eighth again the next year before his success in 1982 put him top of the shop. And, although far removed from the beautiful people who populate the tour, he became a gallery favourite. They identified with the dishevelled, rumpled and high-calorific Stadler who resembled their Sunday morning partner. He was dubbed the 'Walrus' because of his moustache.

He won the first event of the 1982 tour – the Tucson Open – and had three finishes in the top six before the Masters. He won the Kemper again and then beat Ray Floyd in a play-off for the World Series and ended with earnings in the region of 450,000 dollars. Married to Sue with a son, Kevin, Stadler enjoys fishing, skiing and playing the stock market.

Jan Stephenson

Born: December 22, 1951, Sydney, Australia.
Lives: Fort Worth, Texas, U.S.A.
Height: 5–5. *Weight:* 115.
Turned Pro: 1973.
Career Highlights
Australian Championship: 1971.
Naples Classic: 1976.
Birmingham Classic: 1976.
Women's International: 1978.
Sun City Classic: 1980.
Peter Jackson Classic: 1981.
Mary Kay Classic: 1981.
United Virginia Bank Classic: 1981.

One of the most gorgeous women on

Jan Stephenson.

the circuit, the blue-eyed blonde has featured in model magazines as well as in the sports papers. Before moving to America she won four events on the Australian circuit, including the Australian Championship. She was an instant hit in the States and was voted Rookie of the Year in 1974. At the 1981 Mary Kay Classic in Dallas, she set the all-time 54 hole record with rounds of 65–69–64 for an 18-under par total of 198.

Payne Stewart

Born: January 30, 1957, Springfield, Missouri, U.S.A.
Lives: Springfield.
Height: 6–0. *Weight:* 175.
Turned Pro: 1979.
Career Highlights
Quad Cities Open: 1982.
Indian Open: 1981.
Indonesian Open: 1981.

After failing the 1979 autumn school despite a good college career, Stewart found fortune on the Asian tour and claimed victories in the 1981 Indian and Indonesian Opens. He passed the 1981 spring school and gained his first tour victory in the 1982 Quad Cities Open. He was christened with a first name of William, but prefers his more unusual middle name of Payne. Married to Tracey.

Dave Stockton

Born: November 2, 1941, San Bernardino, California, U.S.A.
Lives: Keystone, Colorado and Westlake Village, California.
Height: 5–11. *Weight:* 180.
Turned Pro: 1964.
Career Highlights
U.S. PGA: 1970, 1976.

Cleveland Open: 1968.
Milwaukee Open: 1968, 1973.
Massachusetts Open: 1971.
Los Angeles Open: 1974.
Quad Cities: 1974.
Hartford Open: 1974.
Ryder Cup: 1971, 1977.

Stockton needed his PGA exempt status to stay on the tour during the past three years when he finished way down the money list. He almost gained two other majors, finishing equal second with Tom Weiskopf in the 1974 Masters and tieing for second in the 1978 U.S. Open with J.C. Snead. He has 11 tour victories, 1974 being the highlight with three successes and also his best money year $155,105. The descendant of one of the signaturees of the Declaration of Independence, he was captain of golf at the University of Southern California. A fine ambassador for his sport, his expert technique and easy manner put him in great demand for exhibitions. He loves hunting and fishing and so was delighted to accept the recent post as Director of Golf at the Keystone resort in the Colorado mountain country. Married to Catherine, with two sons.

Curtis Strange

Born: January 30, 1955, Norfolk, Virginia, U.S.A.
Lives: Kingsmill, Virginia.
Height: 5–11. *Weight:* 170.
Turned Pro: 1976.
Career Highlights
Pensacola Open: 1979.
Houston Open: 1980.
Westchester Classic: 1980.
World Amateur Cup: 1974.
Walker Cup: 1975.

Strange played every day from the age of eight and went on to dominate the

Curtis Strange.

amateur scene near his home. Among his victories was the Eastern Amateur in 1975, which his father had won 18 years earlier. It is a mystery why he has not won more than three U.S. tour tournaments. In 1982 he claimed over 236,000 dollars and broke his friend Bill Rogers' record (230,500 dollars in 1979) for the most money earned without a victory. He is comfortably in the top ten money winners, and shared the 36-hole lead in the 1982 Masters before finishing seventh. Married to Sarah.

Ron Streck
Born: July 17, 1954, Tulsa, Oklahoma, U.S.A.
Lives: Tulsa, Oklahoma.
Height: 6–0.   *Weight:* 165.
Turned Pro: 1976.
Career Highlights
San Antonio-Texas Open: 1978.
Michelob-Houston Open: 1981.

When Streck blows hot, stand aside or get burned. He holds the U.S. tour record for the lowest consecutive rounds with 63–62 in the last rounds of the 1978 Texas Open at Oak Hills Country Club. He had another 62 in the third round of the Houston Open in 1981. He gained his first top 60 money finish in 1981. Married to Debbie.

Mike Sullivan
Born: January 1, 1955, Gary, Indiana, U.S.A.
Lives: Ocala, Florida.
Height: 6–2.   *Weight:* 215.
Turned Pro: 1975.
Career Highlight
Southern Open: 1980.

Sullivan qualified for the tour at his third attempt and has found life a struggle with constant swing problems. But he won his first tournament – the Southern Open – by a five stroke margin. He lost the play-off with J.C. Snead for same title the next year. He also lost the play-off with Jack Newton in the Buick Open in 1978. The son of a

Mike Sullivan.

Muriel Thomson.

scratch amateur, Mike studied at the University of Florida. Married to Sandy.

Leonard Thompson
Born: January 1, 1947, Laurinburg, North Carolina, U.S.A.
Lives: Lumberton, North Carolina.
Height: 6–2. *Weight:* 210.
Turned Pro: 1970.
Career Highlights
Jackie-Gleeson-Inverrary Classic: 1974.
Pensacola Open: 1977.

Thompson has a constant fight with the scales and seems to do better with a well-rounded figure. A real crash diet shed 50 pounds in weight but caused a drop from the U.S. top 60 money winners in 1976 with earnings of only 26,500 dollars. Capable of staggerinly low scores, he broke the course record

on the difficult Glen Abbey course in the 1981 Canadian Open with a nine under par 62 (31–31). Married to Lesley, with two children.

Muriel Thomson
Born: December 12, 1954, Aberdeen, Scotland.
Lives: Aberdeen.
Height: 5–5. *Weight:* 133.
Turned Pro: 1979.
Career Highlights
Canadian Foursome: 1978.
Elizabeth Ann Classic: 1981.
Curtis Cup: 1978.

One of triplets, Muriel made an impressive start to her professional career after a distinguished amateur record. She recorded ten top ten finishes in her first season and took this total to 15 when she finished top of the Hambro Life Order of Merit in 1981.

Sam Torrance

Born: August 24, 1953, Largs,
  Scotland.
Lives: Largs.
Height: 6–0. *Weight:* 190.
Turned Pro: 1970.
Career Highlights
Zambian Open: 1975.
Martini International: 1976.
Columbian Open: 1979.
Australian PGA: 1980.
Carrolls Irish Open: 1981.
Spanish Open: 1982.
Ryder Cup: 1981.

Rookie of the Year in 1972, Torrance never lets the grass grow beneath his feet as he travels the world to play all 12 months of the year. His tournament record does not reflect his ability. He clinched his first Ryder Cup place with victory in the 1981 Irish Open but then hit a lean period. He looked set to break the spell when he was five strokes clear with nine holes to go in the 1982 European Open. But the Spaniard Manuel Pinero broke the course record with a furious charge to win by two shots. Other gilt-edged chances went in the PGA and Scandinavian Open, but success came at Madrid where he took the Spanish Open by eight strokes.

Sam Torrance.

Peter Townsend.

Peter Townsend

Born: September 16, 1946, Cambridge, Cambridgeshire, England.
Lives: Dublin, Ireland.
Height: 5–8. *Weight:* 155.
Turned Pro: 1966.
Career Highlights
Dutch Open: ¹967.
Coca Cola Young Professionals: 1968.
Western Australia Open: 1968.
Caracus Open: 1969.
Swiss Open: 1971.
Zambian Open: 1978.
Columbian Open: 1978.
Ryder Cup: 1969, 1971.

Townsend has never fully realised the exciting promise of his amateur career. He won the British Boys' Championship in 1962 and 1964 and then the British Youths' in 1965. His natural style promised him the world when he turned professional after capturing the English Open Stroke Play event. When he won the 1967 Dutch Open it seemed a natural progression, but there were more hiccups than hoorays and his last victory in Britain was the PGA Close Championship in 1968. He equalled the European record of seven successive birdies in one round in the 1974 PGA Championship.

Lee Trevino

Born: December 1, 1939, Dallas,
  Texas, U.S.A.
Lives: Dallas, Texas.
Height: 5–7. *Weight:* 186.
Turned Pro: 1960.
Career Highlights
U.S. Open: 1968, 1971.
British Open: 1971, 1972.
U.S. PGA: 1974.
World Series: 1974.
Hawaiian Open: 1968.
Tucson Open: 1969, 1970.
Tallahassee Open: 1971.
Memphis Classic: 1971, 1972, 1980.
Canadian Open: 1971, 1977, 1979.
Sahara Open: 1971.
Hartford Open: 1972.
St Louis Open: 1972.
Inverrary Classic: 1973.
Doral Eastern: 1973.
Texas Open: 1980.
Tournament of Champions: 1981.
Ryder Cup: 1969, 1971, 1973, 1975,
  1979, 1981.

Trevino was something new. He still
kept a smile on his face even under pressure. His wisecracks delighted the galleries and infuriated some of his fellow
professionals. Eventually his record
had to make them accept him and he
announced his genuine arrival after
years of hustling and near triumphs
with the 1968 U.S. Open. Supermex
was on his way, winning the Tucson in
1969 and 1970 before a staggering
1971. Then as well as tour victories in
the Tallahassee, the Danny Thomas-
Memphis and the Sahara, he annexed a
hat-trick of Open Championships in
the space of 20 days – the U.S., the
Canadian and the British.

He claimed the U.S. PGA in 1974,
but then he was struck by lightning with
Jerry Heard and Bobby Nicholls in the
Western Open at the Butler National
Golf Club, Illinois, in 1975. All three
were rushed to hospital. Trevino later
needed surgery to remove a disc and has
had back problems ever since.

Lee Trevino.

Lee Trevino smiling under pressure.

Although he had a fabulous 1980 with earnings of over 385,000 dollars and a swing average of 69.73 for 82 rounds – lowest since Sam Snead in 1950 – significantly he has not won a major since the lightning incident.

Lee Trevino is one of only five Americans to win the U.S. and British Opens in the same year (the others are Bobby Jones (1926 and 1930), Gene Sarazen (1932), Ben Hogan (1953) and Tom Watson (1982)). Trevino, born of Mexican parents, learned his golf in the U.S. Marine Corps and proved a natural. Married to Claudia, with three children.

Peter Tupling

Born: April 6, 1950, Sheffield,
   Yorkshire, England.
Lives: Sheffield.
Height: 6–2. *Weight:* 182.
Turned Pro: 1969.
Career Highlights
Nigerian Open: 1981.
Walker Cup: 1969.

The 1967 British Boys' Champion has
never been a force on the European
tournament but his name will figure for
all time in the record books. In the
opening event of the 1981 Safari tour,
the Zambian Open, he strung together
rounds of 63–66–62–64 for an aggregate of 255 to beat the previous 72-hole
world record held by America's Mike
Souchak with 257 in the 1955 Texas
Open.

Tommy Valentine

Born: October 21, 1949, Atlanta,
   Georgia, U.S.A.
Lives: Gainesville, Georgia.
Height: 5–11. *Weight:* 175.
Turned Pro: 1974.
Career Highlight
Johnny Miller Invitational: 1980.

Valentine will have to show a marked
improvement if he is to continue to
indulge in his hobby of collecting gold
coins. While at the University of Georgia, he won the national college long-
driving competition and still crashes the
ball a fair way. His best finish was to tie
for first place with Tom Watson in the
1981 Atlanta Classic, but he lost the
play-off.

Bobby Wadkins

Born: July 26, 1951, Richmond,
   Virginia, U.S.A.

Lives: Richmond Virginia.
Height: 6–1. *Weight:* 180.
Turned Pro: 1973.
Career Highlights
Virginia State Amateur: 1971.
European Open: 1978.

Wadkins found the American circuit
hard work after gaining his card in
1974, although he was in the top 60
money earners in 1978 and 1979. He
won the inaugural European Open in
1978 at Walton Heath during the same
week as his elder brother Lanny won
the Garden State PGA in Australia. He
enjoys water-skiing and hunting.

Lanny Wadkins

Born: December 5, 1949, Richmond,
   Virginia, U.S.A.
Lives: Dallas, Texas.
Height: 5–9. *Weight:* 155.
Turned Pro: 1971.
Career Highlights
U.S. PGA: 1977.
World Series: 1977.
Tournament Players' Championship:
   1979.
Sahara Invitational: 1972.
Byron Nelson: 1973.
Los Angeles Open: 1979.
Walker Cup: 1969, 1971.
Ryder Cup: 1977, 1979.

After a brilliant amateur career which
included victory in the 1970 U.S.
Amateur, Wadkins was 1972 Rookie of
the Year when he claimed his first tour
success in the Sahara Invitational.
Surgery for the removal of his gall blad-
der and a hurried return caused a recession in 1975. He won the 1977 U.S.
PGA at the third extra hole after a tie
with Gene Littler.
   His victory in the 1979 Tournament
Players' Championship resulted from a

Lanny Wadkins.

masterful display on a windlashed last day and he finished five strokes ahead of Tom Watson. After moderate years in 1980 and 1981, his winnings picked up again in 1982. Married to Penelope, with a daughter, Dawn.

Brian Waites

Born: March 1, 1940, Bolton, Lancashire, England.
Lives: Nottingham.
Height: 6–1.   *Weight:* 168.
Turned Pro: 1957.

Career Highlights
Tournament Players' Championship: 1978.
Zambian Open: 1979, 1982.
Car Care Plan International: 1982.

Modest Waites made only occasional sorties on to the tournament circuit because he did not think he was good enough. He concentrated on being the model club professional and even now he divides his time equally between the tour and his Hollinwell club job. He claimed his first success on the circuit in

Brian Waites.

1978 with the Tournament Players' Championship.

He has plundered the Safari tour regularly and, after picking up £20,000 by winning the 1982 Zambian and Mufulira Opens, he headed the favourite Sevvy Ballesteros to take the Car Care Plan International at Moor Allerton.

Michelle Walker

Born: December 17, 1952, Leeds, Yorkshire, England.
Lives: Barnet, Hertfordshire.
Height: 5–11. *Weight:* 150.
Turned Pro: 1973.
Career Highlights
British Open: 1971, 1972.
Trans-Mississippi: 1972.

Spanish Open: 1973.
Lambert and Butler Match Play: 1980.
Curtis Cup: 1972.

Michelle had a superb amateur career. She was virtually unbeatable during the two years she won the British Open and was undefeated in her only Curtis Cup appearance. She was the first British woman for 36 years to win an American tournament when she claimed the Trans-Mississippi title in 1972. But the transition to a professional has proved difficult. She was awarded her American card in 1974 but had to re-qualify the next year and headed the school. She lost the play-off for first place in the Jerry Lewis Muscular Dystrophy Classic in 1976.

Michelle Walker.

Tom Watson

Born: September 4, 1949, Kansas City,
Missouri, U.S.A.
Lives: Mission Hills, Kansas.
Height: 5–9.   *Weight:* 162.
Turned Pro: 1971.
Career Highlights
U.S. Open: 1982.
U.S. Masters: 1977, 1981.
British Open: 1975, 1977, 1980, 1982.
World Series: 1975, 1980.
Western Open: 1974, 1977.
Bing Crosby National Pro-Am: 1977,
1978.
San Diego Open: 1977, 1980.
Tucson Open: 1978.
Byron Nelson Classic: 1975, 1978,
1979, 1980.
Hall of Fame Classic: 1978, 1979.
Tournament of Champions: 1979,
1980.
New Orleans Open: 1980, 1981.
Los Angeles Open:1980.
Atlanta Classic: 1982.
Ryder Cup: 1977, 1981.

Watson is the player most likely to
overhaul Jack Nicklaus, although he
was originally labelled a 'choker' after
blowing the 1974 and 1975 U.S.
Opens. He has now demonstrated he
can take the pressure at the head of the
pack. And it could be he has already
overtaken the 'Golden Bear' as the
tour's superstar.

He has certainly put the evil eye on
his rival in their public shoot-outs starting with the U.S. Masters in 1977 and,
the classic head-to-head battle in the
British Open the same year. He did it
again in the 1981 Masters and most
important of all, in the 1982 U.S. Open
at Pebble Beach, when a conjurer's trick
shot at the 71st gave him an improbable
birdie and he rammed in a long putt at
the last just to confirm the situation. It
marked also a change in the quiet man.

His dance around the green after the
superb chip from dangerous greenside
rough into the hole showed the American public real joy. His defences were
down, the inhibitions lifted and the gallery loved it.

He must be the current world
number one. It is not that he cannot be
beaten, but if he plays to his potential he
will head the field. His feat in 1980,
when he won three straight starts and
was never out of the lead through the 12
rounds, was a warning for the next
decade. A Stanford University degree in
psychology suggests he has the mental
ability to handle it. Married to Linda,
with a daughter Meg.

Watson winning the U.S. Open 1982.

Tom Watson.

Tom Watson.

Paul Way

Born: March 12, 1963, Tunbridge
  Wells, Kent, England.
Lives: Kent.
Height: 5–8. *Weight:* 142.
Turned Pro: 1981.
Career Highlights
Dutch Open: 1982.
English Amateur Stroke Play: 1981.
Walker Cup: 1981.

Way became one of the rare rookies who win in their first year, when he took advantage of the absence of several stars to claim the 1982 Dutch Open at Utrecht. He easily achieved his ambition of making the top 60 money earners in his first year. He models himself on Gary Player and runs every morning and does 100 press-ups to build his physique.

D.A. Weibring

Born: May 25, 1953, Quincy, Illinois,
  U.S.A.
Lives: Dallas, Texas.
Height: 6–1. *Weight:* 175.
Turned Pro: 1975.
Career Highlights
Quad Cities Open: 1979.

Weibring uses his initials as he has the same first names – Donald Albert – as his father. He gained his card at his third attempt and has shown steady improvement, moving higher up the money list each year. He claimed his first tour success in the 1979 Quad Cities Open. Now he is in demand for clinics, where he plays straight man to Peter Jacobsen. Married to Kristy, with a son Matt.

Tom Weiskopf

Born: November 9, 1942, Massillon,
  Ohio, U.S.A.
Lives: Paradise Valley, Arizona.
Height: 6–3. *Weight:* 185.

Tom Weiskopf.

Turned Pro: 1964.
Career Highlights
British Open: 1973.
Canadian Open: 1973, 1975.
World Series: 1973.
World Match Play: 1972.
San Diego Open: 1968.
Buick: 1968.
Kemper Open: 1971, 1973, 1977.
Philadelphia Open: 1971, 1973.
Inverrary Classic: 1972.
Greensboro Open: 1975.
Colonial Invitation: 1973.
Argentine Open: 1979.
World Cup team: 1972.
Doral-Eastern: 1978.
La Jet Classic: 1981.
South African PGA: 1973.
Benson and Hedges: 1981.
Ryder Cup: 1973, 1975.

One of the six members of the two million dollar winners' club, Weiskopf's career is often considered a disappointment. The question still asked is what went wrong after 1973. The classic swinger won his first major – the British Open at Troon, the Canadian Open, the World Series and three tournament successes. It seemed he was poised to move out of the shadow of Jack Nicklaus (they are both from Columbus, Ohio) and chase him for the majors. Although handicapped by a hand injury, he found the razmatazz difficult to handle. He still has only 15 U.S. tour victories without another major. Although he denies it, his temperament has played a part and he has been dubbed 'The Towering Inferno' and 'The temper with the shortest fuse.' Age has drawn most of the sting and apparently some of his desire for success too. His victory in the 1981 La Jet Classic in Abilene, Texas, was his first for three and a half years. Married to Jeanne, with two children.

Kathy Whitworth

Born: September 27, 1939, Monahans, Texas, U.S.A.
Lives: Dallas, Texas.
Height: 5–9. *Weight:* 140.
Turned Pro: 1959.
Career Highlights
LPGA Championship: 1967, 1971, 1975.

Arguably the greatest woman golfer of modern times, Kathy was the first to earn more than a million dollars. She has more than 80 tour victories to her credit and was voted Player of the Year seven times between 1966 and 1973. In 1981 she was elected to the Texas Sports Hall of Fame.

Kathy Whitworth.

Ian Woosnam

Born: March 2, 1958, Oswestry,
 Shropshire, England.
Lives: Oswestry.
Height: 5–4. *Weight:* 140.
Turned Pro: 1976.
Career Highlight
Swiss Open: 1982.

Woosnam may be the smallest man of
the European tour but he is now fighting towards the top. He was outside the
top 100 in 1981, but finished in third
place in the Safari tour in the winter and
that gave him automatic entry into the
circuit's events. He certainly benefitted
from not having to pre-qualify,
although his first victory in the 1982
Swiss Open was fairly nerve-racking
before he beat Bill Longmuir at the
third extra hole – the first Briton to win
the tournament for 11 years. He had
been placed second four times in the
previous eight months, twice in Africa,
the Italian Open and the Benson and
Hedges International.

Acknowledgements

Data compiled by David Emery, Randall Northam, Chris Martin, Kevin Francis. Revised by Barry Newcombe.

Photographs by All Sport/Tony Duffy and Bob Martin.